T0347380

FINANCIAL REFORM IN CHINA

China's spectacular economic growth has made it the focus of international attention. *Financial Reform in China* argues that Chinese financial reform has not kept pace with its continuing economic growth.

Written by the leading protagonists of China's financial institutions and markets, *Financial Reform in China* looks at the bottleneck of strict financial regulation which threatens China's continuing economic reform. With increased marketisation and internationalisation, China's financial and monetary system should play a pivotal role in economic reform and development. However, while China's banking and financial organisations still operate under a highly regulated environment shaped by the centrally planned economic system, China's slow financial reform has failed to meet the demands of its more general economic reform.

On Kit Tam is Senior Lecturer in Economics, University of New South Wales, Canberra, Australia.

ROUTLEDGE STUDIES IN THE GROWTH ECONOMIES OF ASIA

FINANCIAL REFORM IN CHINA

Edited by On Kit Tam

London and New York

First published 1995
by Routledge
11 New Fetter Lane, London EC4P 4EE

Reprinted 1997, 1999, 2001

Simultaneously published in the USA and Canada
by Routledge
29 West 35th Street, New York, NY 10001

Routledge is an imprint of the Taylor & Francis Group

© 1995 On Kit Tam

Typeset in Garamond by
J&L Composition Ltd, Filey, North Yorkshire

Printed and bound in Great Britain by
Biddles Ltd, Guildford and King's Lynn

British Library Cataloguing in Publication Data
A catalogue record for this book is available from the British Library

Library of Congress Cataloguing in Publication Data
A catalogue record for this book is available from the Library of Congress

ISBN 0–415–01971–0

CONTENTS

LIST OF FIGURES

LIST OF TABLES

CONTRIBUTORS

On Kit Tam
Senior Lecturer in Economics, the University of New South Wales, Canberra, Australia

Ou Jiawa
Senior banker in a major Chinese state-owned national bank

Wu Jinglian
Deputy Director, Development Centre of the Chinese State Council

Xia Bin
General Manager, Shenzhen Stock Exchange, China

Wu Xiaoling
Director, Policy Research Department, People's Bank of China (central bank)

Huang Yanxin
Head, Economic Adjustment Division, Ministry of Agriculture, China

Gao Xiao Hang
Senior Manager, International Finance Department, Everbright Trust and Investment Corporation of China, Beijing

PREFACE

In contrast to the transition of the former socialist economies in East Europe and Russia, China's gradual approach to economic reform has on the whole been remarkably successful, although it is generally accepted that the experience may not be readily emulated by other reforming economies. One apparent characteristic of this gradual approach is the *ad hoc* nature of the reform process with no master blueprint for a co-ordinated programme. The overall achievements of the reform process should not however be taken to mean that the Chinese approach is without serious problems that can undermine success.

Indeed, in the area of macroeconomic management, the Chinese government has not really been able to exercise effective controls and has resorted often to recentralised direct interventions. The loss of control over the growth of aggregate demand, particularly capital investment financed by the state-owned banking system, and the persistence of destabilising episodes of price inflation are major examples of that problem. After over a decade and a half of economic reform, these macroeconomic issues are still being dealt with via traditional administrative interventions and central commands. The backward financial system is clearly an institutional bottle-neck for the country's continuing growth and a threat to economic stability.

Despite the various systemic changes and new economic institutions that have been introduced, much of China's banking and financial organisations still operate under a highly regulated environment shaped by the centrally planned economic system. It can be argued that a key problem in China's macroeconomic management is the slow progress in transforming the country's financial system. With increasing marketisation and internationalisation, the financial and monetary system should play a pivotal role in the country's continuing economic reform and development. However, fundamental reform of the financial system has not been significant and has not kept pace with the demands that come with the progress of general economic reform. In the areas of money, banking and credits there remain major rigidities and inconsistencies in the way they are allowed to operate, which should be in an appropriately supervised market-oriented environment – a necessary condition for other key reforms and for maintaining economic stabilitiy.

This volume aims to provide a better understanding of the reform of China's financial system by focusing on the key institutional aspects of the transformation process. While the Chinese reform is a gradual process, this does not mean that there has been a lack of considered thoughts, particularly among Chinese economists, on the grander visions and specific strategies. Most of the Chinese contributors to this volume have actively participated in the formulation of ideas and high-level policy advice. Indeed, some of them have at various stages been directly involved in the development and creation of China's new financial institutions and markets. It is hoped that this volume will, through its analysis of the reform of the financial system using information up to about 1992, shed some light on the deeper financial and monetary causes of the persistent problems in China's macroeconomic management.

On Kit Tam
The University of New South Wales, Canberra

ACKNOWLEDGEMENTS

I wish to thank Ms Peng Xiao Meng for her invaluable assistance in liaising with contributors in China and in providing very effective logistical support for research in Beijing. Thanks are also due to Dr Yang Gang and Mr Li Yongping for research assistance and to Ms Jill Kenna for her very efficient word processing. My research is supported in part by a grant from the Australian Research Council and is gratefully acknowledged. Some chapters were written by contributors before they took up their current positions. Views expressed in this volume are the individual contributors' and do not represent the views of the organisations with which they are currently or previously associated.

On Kit Tam

1

MONETARY MANAGEMENT AND FINANCIAL REFORM

On Kit Tam

1 INTRODUCTION

China's economic reform process has changed in fundamental ways the basic structures of its economic system. The non-state economic sector is now producing over 50 per cent of the country's output and the share of the households in national saving jumped from 24 per cent in 1979 to 71 per cent in 1991.[1] However, the Chinese financial sector is still dominated by banks and financial institutions owned and run by the state, primarily to serve the government and the ailing state-owned enterprises. The four state-owned specialised banks accounted for over three-quarters of the assets of the country's bank and non-bank financial institutions in 1992.[2] The urban and rural credit co-operatives, which together accounted for another 13 per cent of the total assets, are practically run by their 'supervising' state-owned banks (the Industrial and Commercial Bank of China and the Agricultural Bank of China, respectively).

The Chinese economy today has achieved rapid growth as well as a high degree of openness by historical and international standards. The role of the market is being restored to an increasing range of economic activities. Money, credit and banking are entering a new phase of importance in the determination of production, consumption, investment and exchanges in China. However, the Chinese government still has few effective market-based policy instruments and continues to rely on direct administrative commands to exercise control over the economy. The perennial concerns about the overheating of the economy, the threats of uncontrollable inflation, the 'shortage' of funds and the rising budget deficits are but a few of a growing list of

1

indications that Chinese monetary management under the partially reformed economic system is assuming much greater significance and faces uncharted challenges, but the performance seems less than reassuring.

It is now widely accepted among the more informed observers of the reforming centrally planned economies that simply transposing from mature market economies some facets of their organisations and institutions is neither sufficient nor appropriate for what is in effect the transformation of an entire economic, political and social system. Regardless of the strategies on how China's financial system should be reformed and developed, any realistic analysis of its monetary transformation should be based on an understanding of the mechanisms and institutions that shape the fundamental processes of money supply and demand. This study will address this important but often neglected area by examining China's monetary and financial planning mechanisms to explain why the Chinese government cannot exercise effective monetary control unless the present financial and banking system is fundamentally transformed and monetary unification achieved. It rejects the suggestion that the reform of the banking system is separate from, and can therefore await the successful completion of, reform in the tax system and the 'liberalisation' of state enterprises.[3]

How well the Chinese government can tackle the management of the rapidly developing financial and monetary system will have a major impact on the success of the reform and development in other areas. However, despite the rapidly growing literature on many areas of the Chinese economic reform, there is in general a lack of appreciation of the significance of the institutions and real processes of money, credits and monetary control in this transitory economic system. Although there are now many relevant works on key aspects of China's money and finance,[4] the findings and insights they have produced seldom find their way into other studies of the Chinese economy. Often analytical models on the Chinese economy are based on an implicit assumption that money does not matter, so that the institutions and mechanism through which money is created and demanded are accorded even less importance. Other studies of the Chinese economic reform may take some new institutions and activities that resemble, on cursory examination, those found in market economies as having the same functions in China. Thus, the establishment of a central bank, the

2

introduction of regulations regarding bank reserve requirements, or the creation of inter-bank money markets are sometimes interpreted to mean, for example, that the concept of high-powered money and money multiplier can be applied to Chinese monetary management.

This chapter will show that effective monetary management through market-based instruments and procedures is becoming more urgent but is yet far from being achieved. Despite the facade of a partially reformed financial system and the higher degree of internationalisation of the economy, monetary management in China is still essentially reliant on the traditional discretionary administrative commands and interventions. The primacy of the national financial planning mandates and a non-unified (segmented) money are two major causes of the difficulties in China's monetary management. This chapter presents an analytical framework that incorporates the basic characteristics of Chinese financial planning and the segmented money system to explain the problems of monetary management in a changing economic system, an approach that has not been attempted in previous studies on the subject. Because Chinese monetary management has primarily been domestically focused with the extensive foreign exchange controls in place, this study will limit its analysis to domestic monetary issues. This does not mean, however, that the impacts of China's expanding participation in international finance are insignificant. Indeed, as will be discussed, the progress of the economic reform and opening-up process is fast negating the relevance of the traditional monetary approach. The question of exchange controls is examined in another chapter of this book.

The Chinese economy, having embarked on the road back to a market economy, cannot be expected to operate efficiently without a market-based financial and banking system that allows risk-taking and is subject to the exercise of prudential monetary controls. More fundamental changes to the outdated mode of monetary management inherited from the days of centralised planning are inevitable. Clearly the ultimate success of financial reform will be dependent on progress in other key areas of reform such as the mode of public sector finance, state enterprise transformation and the creation of a more independent central bank and an autonomous commercial banking industry. On the basis of the analysis of this study, some immediate policy options can none the less be considered. They include: allowing the four state-owned specialised banks to break up, merge and re-organise to improve their performance; abolishing the segmented monetary flow system for cash and enterprise money; allowing individuals to operate cheque accounts, and enterprises/organisations to hold and use cash; establishing a modern bank clearing national network; and, subject to some asset and performance requirements, removing barriers to entry for new domestic and foreign banks and financial institutions.

Section 2 of this chapter examines the role of money in the Chinese economy. It discusses the concept and function of money segmentation as an institutional and organisational structure of the Chinese economic system. Section 3 presents an analytical model of China's financial and monetary planning. Section 4 discusses how the financial reform has impacted on the efficacy of the model. It examines the problem of the state budget process from the perspective of China's framework of financial planning. It shows that the two pillars of China's financial planning and monetary management, the credit plan and the cash plan, have become completely ineffectual and dysfunctional instruments for the purpose of instituting market-based policy measures. Section 5 outlines a number of policy options and provides some conclusions.

2 MONEY IN THE CHANGING CHINESE ECONOMIC SYSTEM

Given the importance and complexity of a country's financial system, its development and reform often require commensurate changes in other key areas of the economy to make it work. Financial reform involves both institution-building with innovations as well as a broader transformation of the role of the government, including subsets of financial deregulation and liberalisation.[5] For a centrally planned economy that is being reformed to become more open and market-oriented, the reform of its financial and monetary system should clearly be an integral part of the process of the systemic change.

China's financial reform of the 1980s really began as an intermediate goal mandated to give effect to the new financial demands arising from its enterprise and fiscal reforms and the changing output and ownership structures of the economy. Because China's economic reform has been a partial and gradual process,

4

financial reform measures have often been carried out in an *ad hoc* and piecemeal fashion to achieve a variety of objectives, some of which are not necessarily compatible.

Indeed, some observers, both Western and Chinese, have attributed the Chinese government's poor performance in macroeconomic and monetary controls to the financial reform.[6] It is important, therefore, to understand the real nature of the financial reform and the associated mechanism through which economic stability has been affected. McKinnon (1992, p. 121) has rightly pointed out that:

> because the nature of monetary and fiscal processes in the 'classical' Stalinist centrally planned economy was not (and is not) well understood by people who are familiar only with financial mechanisms in mature industrial economies, well-meaning advice and enthusiasm by outsiders for liberalization can easily be misguided.

Since China's financial and monetary reforms have from the beginning been intertwined with changes in the systems of resource allocation, public finance and the management and control of the vast state enterprise sector, it is indeed vital to understand the fundamental characteristics of the changing financial and monetary processes so that a more realistic assessment and policy recommendation can be made.

It is clear that monetary management is central to the achievement of macroeconomic stability and sustained growth in China. This study will show, however, that the present ineffectual centralised system of money and credit controls must be discontinued as it is no longer compatible with the new economic institutions and money behaviour. One of the keys to the achievement of this goal is to establish an independent banking system that is not run as a part of the government, so that the automatic monetisation of the imbalances in government spending and revenue, whether in open or disguised form, can be discontinued. In addition, it is becoming increasingly urgent to unify the formally segmented cash and non-cash money. A complete monetary transformation is necessary.

Centrally planned economies have for a long time relied on a system of direct controls that are predicated on separating production and consumption activities through the use of different monies. Cash is retricted primarily to the household sector for income and consumption purposes, and transfer money (bank deposits operable primarily through transfers between accounts) for the non-household sectors for all inter-enterprise and inter-government transactions. The two segregated monetary flows form an integral part of the centralised command system for facilitating the planned mobilisation and allocation of resources. A monobanking system is established to implement the financial and monetary plans that are drawn up to meet the targets in the economic plan in physical terms.

The monobank is not really a commercial bank at all in the convention of modern market economies. It acts as the government's receiver of monies, cashier and an administrative organ for the implementation of central plans. The government has believed that the segmentation of money would facilitate the implementation of a Stalinist industrialisation drive through a centralised system of resource allocation supported by the separate control of the volume of the two monies. The reality was that the segmentation had never been complete. For instance, increase in transfer money in enterprise deposits may ultimately be used to expand employment, thereby raising the amount of cash money needed to pay the additional wage cost. The common belief that centrally planned economies have had total control of their money and that money did not matter under that system is unfounded.

In transforming China's financial and banking systems to meet the emerging demands of the economic reform process, it is therefore important to address both the question of how the new system be restructured,[7] as well as the issue of ending the separation of the dual money system and the associated planning and control mechanisms. Unfortunately, that latter issue has attracted little attention.[8] While the recently announced plan to establish development banks may ease to some extent the problems with the hidden loan subsidies imposed on the specialised banks, the fundamental issues arising from the continuation of the formal framework for national financial planning and the dichotomisation of money flows, and the problem of the establishment of independence and market disciplines in the banking system, are not therefore necessarily resolved.

The notion of unification has always been considered desirable by the Chinese government in its many political and economic endeavours. In China's gradual process of economic reform, however, there are a number of important areas in which unification is clearly needed before the benefits of reforms can be fully realised and sustained. One vital area is monetary unification.

Because of various mobility obstacles and entry barriers, many products and inputs are yet to have national markets, although progress in this area is evident in recent years.[9] Dual or multiple prices for some key commodities and resources (including foreign exchange up to 1993) still exist. However, one area where unification is now urgently needed but generally ignored is the ending of the institution of the artificial segmentation of cash and non-cash money. The Chinese monetary management framework, national financial planning and its banking system continue to operate under the traditional centrally planned model which restricts the use of cash to the household sector for consumption and the use of non-cash money ('transfer money' or 'enterprise money') to the non-household sector for production, investment and most government activities.[10]

With the rapidly expanding role of the market in the country's economic activities, the maintenance of the formal arrangements for monetary segmentation is undermining the fundamental basis through which market-based economic calculations and transactions are made. The developing linkages between saving and investment, and among the households, enterprises and the government are thus distorted and impaired. Without monetary unification, it is not possible to achieve a sound basis for the country's financial reform and the management of its macroeconomy in the new era. It should be noted that the formal institution of money segmentation does not imply in reality that the two types of money can in no way be linked. Indeed, it is precisely because of the fact that complete money segmentation has in reality never been achieved and that the formal institution for the segmentation is now creating more distortions and difficulties for monetary control, that this problem must be resolved. This chapter argues that a fundamental transformation of China's monetary and banking system cannot be delayed if growth and stability are to be attained. The formal unification of the two segmented monies, with all its associated institutions and complementary measures, is overdue and should be implemented immediately.

Monetary management during the pre-reform years was, as a result of money segmentation, dichotomised into controlling cash in circulation and allocating bank credits to support state industrial and commercial enterprises according to national plans. In practice, the objective of monetary management in respect of cash was to be achieved through an annual cash plan that tried to maintain stability in some notional numerical relation between currency in circulation and various measures of retail sales. In conceptual terms, this approach to currency control is implicitly based on the quantity theory of money.[11]

However, it is important to note that, other than a central plan for bank credit targets, there was really no systematic framework to deal with the non-cash transfer money (in the form of bank deposits by enterprises, collectives and government organisations) other than the requirement that withdrawal could only be made for designated uses and that cash withdrawals were strictly limited and controlled. Instead, the management of bank credit allocation was the primary concern of the government and was implemented through the credit plan. The primary policy concern then was to ensure that bank credits, mainly for working capital loans to state enterprises and collectives, and for state procurement of agricultural output, were supplied and used according to the central plan. Therefore, China's monetary management during the pre-reform years was essentially about controlling the narrow definition of money supply through its cash plan.

The rapid development in financial innovation and deregulation in industrialised market economies during the last two decades has led to a re-examination of the concept and definition of money as debates over the stability in the relationship between monetary and other macroeconomic aggregates continue. There is evidence to suggest that significant institutional changes can result in what we think of as money.[12]

With the market-oriented reform of its economy and financial system, the Chinese government has advocated the exercise of more effective macroeconomic management through 'indirect levers' such as monetary and fiscal policies. Meanwhile, China has introduced major institutional changes in its financial system. A better understanding of how they may impact on the meaning of money, its demand behaviour and supply processes would be vital to the success of effective macroeconomic management in the reform process.

There have been a number of recent works that attempt to establish in a reduced form a functional relationship between some measures of money (usually currency) and prices in the

Chinese economy.[13] They are concerned with household money demand, consumer goods market disequilibrium and the methodology of constructing a price index for testing the relationship between prices, cash supply and household income. However, most of these works focus only on cash and do not incorporate considerations of the actual process and institutions through which money control is attempted.[14]

In any analysis of money in a centrally planned economy, the issue of the theoretical concept and empirical definition of monetary aggregate is a particularly important, though often neglected, one. The reason for paying special attention to this issue here is that the governments of such economies have historically reshaped money and their monetary system to serve the requirements of the central planning mechanism so that the concept and functions of money are distorted and changed. Ultimately, a workable empirical definition of money depends on its conceptual functions.[15]

The major functions of money in a market economy include its role as a unit of account, as a medium of exchange (for facilitating transactions and representing purchasing power) and as a store of value (asset). In the case of the Chinese monetary system, the two segmented monies (currency and 'transfer money') do not perform fully those functions. Clearly both serve as a unit of account, but their role as medium of exchange is limited to their respectively designated types of transactions with restriction. For instance, currency is a medium of exchange in the purchase of consumption goods only when supply is available. In the case of the non-household units' bank deposits, they can only be used to settle their approved transactions through a designated single-cheque account[16] with the state-owned monobank (the People's Bank of China before the economic reform). As a store of value, currency can be held for future purchases of a range of consumption goods and selected agricultural inputs, subject to availability; while transfer money basically cannot be used as an asset because of the planned nature of the supply of non-consumption goods and the fact that few alternative forms of assets exist.

In essence, central planning and the use of transfer money are meant to *replace the use* of narrow money (currency) in the non-household sectors (which are only allowed to hold a minimum amount of cash). The major sources of transfer money for the country's production enterprises, collectives and government organisations consist mainly of budget grant allocation and the bank deposits created by government-directed bank credits.[17]

The two types of money are not substitutes. Hence, if we adopt the conventional definition of monetary aggregates in market economies such as M_1 (currency plus checking account [i.e. currency and transfer money]) or M_2 (M_1 plus savings deposits), the vital distinction between these segmented monies can be lost and any explanation of their demand or velocity behaviour will be conceptually difficult to construct and reconcile.[18]

The segmentation of the two money circuits is in practice breaking down rapidly in an asymmetric way under the reform process. Unfortunately, the formal regulations, financial planning mechanism and the institutions associated with the segmented money circuits remain. Since 1978, currency's functions as a medium of exchange (and purchasing power) and store of value have been expanding rapidly from the realm of consumption to investment, and into the producer-goods market as state controls over the economy are gradually relaxed and as the size of the non-state sector grows. At the same time, official restrictions over the use of (non-cash) transfer money are basically intact so that its money functions do not go through a similar significant transformation as currency has done. However, as will be discussed in section 4, with increasing operational and financial autonomy given to state enterprises and sub-national governments, there are a growing number of ways by which transfer money can be converted into the currency circuit to take advantage of the latter's newly acquired money functions. The breaking down of money segmentation on a rising scale has significant implications for the development of the financial system, money supply mechanism, money demand and the conduct of monetary policy in China.[19] It is, however, necessary to understand first how Chinese planners and the monetary authorities operated and how money and finance function under a system of money segmentation, so that the resolution of the problems of a partially reformed financial system can be better approached.

The three basic elements of the traditional mechanism of China's financial and monetary management were the cash plan, the credit plan and the state budget. This chapter presents a simple model to capture their interrelationship under the country's comprehensive fiscal-credit funds planning framework[20] (hereafter referred to as CFP). While the cash plan, and to some extent the credit plan, have quite justifiably received most of the attention in studies on China's monetary system, their relationship to the overall financial planning and monetary management scheme is not often well understood.[21] One of the problems is that the Chinese government has never published official figures and the contents of its CFP. On the basis of the now more widely available Chinese material and this author's field research, quantitative estimates of the major components of the CFP are presented in Table 1.1 (p. 14). The analytical model incorporating the relationship between total state expenditures (E, comprising all budget expenditures, and expenditures by state enterprises and government organisations), state budget revenue (B), the credit plan (L) and the cash plan (C) is given in the section below.

3 CHINESE MODEL OF FINANCIAL PLANNING AND MONETARY MANAGEMENT

Under China's central planning and monobanking system, the supply of transfer money is determined, as will be shown here, by the requirements of the physical and credit plans.[22] Bank credits are simply created as accounting units without reference to bank deposits and are treated as a pre-determined source of funds to finance public sector expenditures including the underwriting of the operating costs of state industrial and commercial enterprises. Chinese policy-makers and economists have always placed their monetary policy focus on currency in circulation since most have defined cash as money supply. However, this study will also show that the narrowly defined money supply (cash) in China is in reality demand determined and plays an accommodating role to rises in the price level and real output.[23]

With a centralised system of resource allocation and comprehensively regulated prices before the economic reform, the cash plan was primarily aimed at maintaining some tolerable balance between monetary purchasing power and the supply of consumption goods. In the general scheme of the CFP before the reform, dependance was placed on state budget (including extra-budget) funds, while bank credits played only a relatively minor supporting role during those years. A monobanking system functions as an agent for implementing the financial counterpart flows of the physical plan. Complex financial planning arrangements linking the state budget, bank lending and currency supply are employed to achieve that end. The CFP model presented here attempts to capture the basic macroeconomic elements and interrelations built into China's actual process of financial and monetary planning:

$$B + L = E \qquad (1)$$
$$L = D + C + A \qquad (2)$$
$$C = J - W \qquad (3)$$

where

$B =$ planned annual state budget income (including extra-budgetary revenue);
$B = BR + XR$
$BR =$ consolidated budget revenues
$XR =$ extra-budgetary revenues

$L =$ planned annual bank lending (including central bank's loans to the government, and receipts from foreign loans)

$E =$ planned annual state expenditures in the economic plan (including repayment of foreign loans and external aid expenditures). It is the sum of budget and extrabudgetary expenditures, and all expenditures by state enterprises and organisations not funded in the form of a grant through the state budget

$D =$ planned annual change in aggregate bank deposits

$C =$ planned annual change in currency in circulation

$A =$ planned annual change in the sum of banks' own capital, banks' bond holding, the banking system's liabilities to international financial institutions and other (including funds in transit)

$A = S_B + S_{INT} + S_K + S_{OTH}$ (see Table 1.2)

$J =$ planned injection of currency in circulation

$W =$ planned withdrawal of currency from circulation

Equation (1) represents the planning principle that expenditures in the state sector are to be funded through the combined funds from budget grants and bank credits in a centralised command economic system.[24] The Chinese government had often declared its desire to achieve separate balances in the state budget, extra-budget and bank finance while attempting to achieve an overall balance in the funding and expenditures of the entire state sector. While in principle the central planners would set targets for all revenues and expenditures items, a complex process of negotiation and bargaining between the planners, ministries and the provincial governments would in practice decide the outcomes of the targets.

The two variables, B and L, on the left-hand side of equation (1), represent the two formal funding mechanisms. B is the expected sum of budget income (BR) and extra-bugetary income (BX) in the state's consolidated (central and local government) account, whereas L represents funds to be supplied from the *credit plan*. Therefore, in terms of revenue in China's national financial planning, the sum of fiscal resources (within and outside the state budget) and bank credits are treated as the source of finance for total state expenditures (central and local, budgetary, extrabudgetary and off-budget items).

The significance of such a macroeconomic management and planning approach is that it created a basis for the credit plan (underwritten by the central bank) to have the potential to become a major source of state finance, as it did during the Great Leap Forward years and increasingly so in the 1980s (Table 1.1). Under this system bank credits are a predetermined source of funds to finance state expenditures, including the underwriting of the operating costs of state-owned industrial and commercial enterprises. Therefore, policy changes brought under the economic reform process to each individual components such as budget reforms and new extrabudgetary arrangements, cannot by themselves alter the institutional basis and outcomes of the Chinese financial planning and management.

Despite its obvious important macroeconomic and monetary management implications, the CFP is not well understood. Indeed, financial management in China has been traditionally more closely identified with controlling the state budget and the cash plan. Unfortunately, the responsibilities for implementing these plans came under different ministries and were not well co-ordinated. On the basis of recently published official statistics on the state budgets, the banking system's liabilities and assets and selected unpublished realised figures of the CFP for 1980–5, estimates of the percentage share of the major funding components of the CFP can be made and are presented in Table 1.1.

Several trends are evident. First, before the economic reform, the proportion of funds contributed by bank credits was low (except in the turbulent years of the Great Leap Forward and its aftermath), as could be expected under a centralised system of payments and receipts where bank credits played a minor role.

Table 1.1 Source of funds in China's CFP (percentage share)

Year	BR	XR	L
1953	85.97	3.59	10.44
1954	78.77	4.42	16.81
1955	87.37	5.82	6.81
1956	86.51	6.38	7.10
1957	81.64	6.93	11.43
1958	60.27	8.70	31.03
1959	54.23	10.75	35.02
1960	67.28	13.85	18.87
1961	142.22	22.93	−65.15
1962	120.56	24.47	−45.02
1963	118.71	17.98	−36.70
1964	82.41	13.58	4.0
1965	76.67	12.23	11.10
1966	74.68	10.84	14.48
1967	77.22	15.40	7.38
1968	67.77	14.52	17.71
1969	77.73	12.90	9.37
1970	78.73	11.99	9.28
1971	78.88	12.56	8.56
1972	81.87	14.34	3.79
1973	72.20	17.06	10.74
1974	71.50	20.06	8.44
1975	69.36	21.39	9.25
1976	68.51	24.29	7.20
1977	66.23	23.66	10.11
1978	68.14	21.10	10.77
1979	59.09	25.07	15.84
1980	50.56	27.04	22.40
1981	49.13	29.07	21.80
1982	46.44	34.39	19.18
1983	45.10	36.04	18.86
1984	37.61	30.47	31.93
1985	42.03	35.00	22.97
1986	38.60	30.70	30.69
1987	37.39	33.53	29.07
1988	39.05	35.61	25.33
1989	37.19	35.27	27.54
1990	34.37	29.70	35.93
1991	32.83	31.04	36.13

Source: Almanac of China's Finance and Banking 1990, pp. 48–53; Statistical Yearbook of China 1991, p. 222; Statistical Yearbook of China 1993, pp. 230, 664.

Second, the state budget (both within and extrabudgetary) played the dominant role in supplying funds to state expenditure requirements. It is also clear that, despite more recent concerns expressed over the relative decline in the share of budgetary resources, the share of extra-budgetary funds has in fact been steadily rising from as early as the mid 1960s. At the start of the economic reform, extrabudgetary funds already accounted for about a quarter of the total funding source of the CFP.

Equation (2) shows the planning relationship between China's two primary monetary management tools, the credit plan and the cash plan. Under a centralised command system, the management of the annual increase in total bank lending is based on the credit plan. Before the reform, bank credits were granted automatically to state enterprises in accordance with the targets (contained in the national economic plan), mainly for financing state enterprises' working capital requirements, agricultural procurement and retail sales. The basis on which bank loans were extended was not based on the level of bank deposits or reserves. Chinese banks did not and still do not operate on a fractional reserve system with a real role for high-powered money. Indeed, equation (2) shows that, under the planning framework, the planned volume of bank lending is set *a priori* to be the sum of the planned increase of currency in circulation (C), planned growth in all bank deposits (D), and the aggregate of banks' own capital, bond issues, overseas liabilities and funds in transit (A). As the share of (A) has remained insignificant over the years (Table 1.2), the size of bank credits is therefore primarily linked to the growth in the volume of household savings deposits plus non-cash transfer money (i.e. D) and currency in circulation (C).

Bank loans to state enterprises and government units are earmarked for approved spending programmes. Such spending must be effected through transfers in their bank accounts with the state-owned banking system. No currency could be withdrawn out of such loans except for approved payment of wages and procurement of agricultural output. The amount of bank lending is not affected by the bank's cash reserve or holding. Thus, as equation (2) indicates, the planned level of bank lending to enterprises and organisations is in fact based on the combined change in the liabilities of the entire banking system[25] (i.e. the central bank and the commercial banks), plus the commercial banks' nominal 'self-owned capital'. Under such a framework, changes in total bank

Table 1.2 Actual yearly change in total bank lending and percentage shares of source of funds

Year	L^*	D	C	S_B	S_{INT}	S_K	S_{OTH}
1953	25.9	55	46	0	0	19	−20
1954	54.1	83	3	0	0	9	4
1955	19.9	−54	−5	0	0	25	134
1956	23.5	−32	72	0	0	52	8
1957	43.4	72	−10	0	0	37	1
1958	199.6	65	8	0	0	21	6
1959	314.5	33	2	0	0	63	2
1960	160.5	38	13	0	0	47	2
1961	−163.1	−18	−18	0	0	114	22
1962	−117.1	68	16	0	0	−15	31
1963	−105.8	−4	16	0	0	−27	115
1964	19.4	131	−51	0	0	−655	674
1965	68.6	60	16	0	0	6	18
1966	108.3	67	16	0	0	16	0
1967	40.1	54	33	0	0	53	−40
1968	94.4	53	13	0	0	22	12
1969	63.5	26	5	0	0	42	27
1970	78.1	80	−17	0	0	35	2
1971	80.8	78	16	0	0	−84	90
1972	35.5	25	42	0	0	−38	71
1973	120.6	74	12	0	0	37	−23
1974	92.4	35	11	0	0	43	11
1975	108.8	71	6	0	0	33	−10
1976	81.6	4	26	0	0	55	15
1977	133.0	64	−6	0	0	43	−1
1978	177.2	40	9	0	0	35	16
1979	286.1	72	19	0	0	17	−8
1980	461.7	70	17	0	7	6	1
1981	450.8	83	11	0	3	6	−3
1982	447.7	77	10	0	0	12	2
1983	506.5	83	18	0	0	9	−10
1984	1245.4	64	21	0	1	4	10
1985	1004.2	68	19	1	1	8	2
1986	1736.9	63	13	1	3	5	15
1987	1759.0	66	13	2	3	7	8
1988	1614.9	56	42	1	−2	8	−5
1989	2076.7	76	10	0	0	6	8
1990	3275.9	81	9	0	1	0	9
1991	3776.1	85	14	1	0	4	−4

Source: Chinese Financial Statistics 1952–87, p. 9; Almanac of China's Finance and Banking 1990, pp. 52–53, 1991, p. 43

lending (L) are linked, *inter alia*, to the planned increase in currency in circulation (C) held by the public *outside the banking system*. As far as the banks are concerned, whether before or after the reform, their credit management has essentially been separated from the management of cash and deposits because of the compulsory nature of plan targets. Table 1.2 presents data on the actual relative shares of each major funding source for the annual flow of all bank credits.

It is clear that bank deposits have been for most years the major source of bank credits. This outcome is not surprising given that, under China's centralised planning system, bank deposit (transfer money) creation is very much a product of the system of passive (automatic) provision of bank credits to state enterprises and government units. That mode of credit provision is also the reason for the lack of financial discipline in state enterprises and in banks.

On the basis of the estimates in Table 1.2, self-owned capital of the banking system may appear to have been another important 'source' of credit funds prior to the economic reform. However, two important qualifications should be noted. First, the level of such funds has suffered huge cut-backs in 1961, 1964 and 1971. Thus, its contributory share in the outstanding balance (as against the data on the annual flows in Table 1.2) of total lending has remained at below 20 per cent for most pre-reform years. Second, Chinese bank capital as a 'source' of credit fund is often illusory as these funds are usually allocated by the Ministry of Finance under the state budget. Funds for such allocations are made *ex post* by two alternative methods.[26] They could be made available at the end of

---

Note: * Unit of measurement for L: 100 million yuan.
All figures (except *L*) are in percentage, i.e. share of total increase (minus sign for decrease) in all sources of funds. Percentages may not add up to 100 per cent because of rounding.

L = $D + C + S_B + S_{INT} + S_K + S_{OTH}$
L = Annual increase (minus sign for decrease) in total bank lending (100 million yuan at current prices)
D = Total deposits
C = currency in circulation
A = $S_B + S_{INT} + S_K + S_{OTH}$
S_B = Banks' bond issues
S_{INT} = Liabilities to international financial institutions
S_K = Banks' own capital
S_{OTH} = Other funds

17

Table 1.3 Bank deposits and composition

Year	DD	Sav + Rur	Ent + Oth
1952	93.3	9	91
1953	107.6	12	88
1954	152.5	12	88
1955	141.7	16	84
1956	134.1	23	77
1957	165.5	28	72
1958	295.3	21	79
1959	398.7	24	76
1960	459.8	22	78
1961	488.7	20	80
1962	409.6	15	85
1963	414	17	83
1964	439.5	21	79
1965	481	21	79
1966	553.6	22	78
1967	575.1	22	78
1968	625.1	23	77
1969	641.7	22	78
1970	704.3	21	79
1971	767.6	22	78
1972	776.3	23	77
1973	865	23	77
1974	897.5	26	74
1975	975.1	26	74
1976	978.5	26	74
1977	1063.8	26	74
1978	1134.5	27	73
1979	1339.1	30	70
1980	1661.2	31	69
1981	2027.4	31	69
1982	2369.9	33	67
1983	2788.6	35	65
1984	3583.9	32	68
1985	4264.9	35	65
1986	5354.7	38	62
1987	6517	41	59
1988	7425.8	45	55
1989	9013.9	49	51
1990	11644.9	52	48
1991	14864.1	54	46

Source: Chinese Financial Statistics 1952–87, pp. 22–25; *Almanac of China's Finance and Banking 1991*, p. 42, 1992, p. 457.

Notes: DD = Total deposits outstanding (end of year balance, 100 million yuan)
Sav + Rur = Percentage share of saving and rural deposits
Ent + Oth = Percentage share of enterprise and other deposits

the financial year only if there is a surplus in the state budget. Alternatively, such funds could be budgeted at the beginning of the plan year and be allocated by the MOF subsequently. More recently, banks are allowed to keep a small unspecified share of their retained net income to build their capital base. Therefore, the importance of banks' own capital is more apparent than real.

Table 1.3 presents data on the relative shares of enterprise and government unit deposits (mainly transfer money) and household deposits (which can easily be converted into currency). Prior to the reform, non-household deposits accounted for over three-quarters of the total outstanding bank deposits. After the reform, the share of household deposits has risen rapidly. As will be discussed below, this change has quite significant implications for monetary management.

While the right-hand side of equation (2) shows the planned 'sources' of funds for total bank credits, their levels are ultimately governed by the planned credit target (L) required to meet the financing need for all state expenditures (E). Because of the imposed separation of consumption and production activities between the household and non-household sectors, and the accompanying segmentation of money into cash and transfer money, the Chinese monetary authority has traditionally concentrated its attention on the management of cash supply in an attempt to ensure price stability in the consumer goods market. The operational intermediate objective is to maintain a desired balance between cash injection and withdrawal through the state banking system to achieve a planned rate of growth in cash supply.

The control of cash withdrawal/injection is to be implemented on the basis of a cash plan (as represented by equation (3)). The major components of cash injection are given below in equation (4), while equation (5) shows the major components of cash withdrawal for a given period. Substituting equation (4) and equation (5) into equation (3) gives equation (6), which represents the cash plan in its withdrawal/injection components.

$$J = WA + PR + SJ + RCJ + GE + ORJ \qquad (4)$$

$$W = RT + FE + SW + RCW + TX + ORW \qquad (5)$$

$$\begin{aligned} C = \ &\{(WA + PR + SJ) - (RT + FE + SW)\} \\ &+ (RCJ - RCW) + (GE - TX) \\ &+ (ORJ - ORW) \end{aligned} \qquad (6)$$

where J = planned injection of currency in circulation

W = planned withdrawal of currency in circulation

WA = wages, bonds and transfer payments to workers

PR = payment of state procurement of agricultural products

SJ = money withdrawal from household saving deposit accounts

RCJ = money withdrawal from rural credit co-operatives' deposit accounts with the state bank

GE = the sum of cash expenditures (by withdrawing cash from bank accounts) by government units and organisations, rural enterprises and organisations and individual businesses

ORJ = the cashing of remittance funds, other cash expenditures and foreign exchange

RT = retail sales of consumer goods including sales of some agricultural inputs

FE = sales of services, fees and charges

SW = money deposited into household saving deposit accounts

RCW = money deposited into rural credit co-operatives' deposit accounts with the state bank

TX = taxes paid in cash (including fines, licence fees and rents), plus cash deposited into state bank accounts by rural enterprises and individual businesses

ORW = depositing of remittance funds, and other cash receipts deposited with the banking system

In reality, the Chinese monetary authority has generally not been successful in the implementation of the cash plan and in controlling the change in cash supply. It is because it could not exercise effective control over changes in the level of the key components in the cash plan (as represented by equation (6)). In terms of cash injection, figures in Table 1.4 indicate that wage payments (WA), agricultural procurement (PR) and household bank deposit withdrawal (SJ) are the most important factors in quantitative terms before the reform. However, it has long been recognised that the monetary authority can exercise little control and influence over these components. With the money wage rate virtually fixed for a long period of time until the economic reform, total wage payments depended on changes in total employment over which the monetary authority had little direct influence. Cash payment for state procurement of agricultural goods is a function of the actual harvested output, a variable neither the central bank nor the central planning commission could control. As far as household bank deposit withdrawal (SJ) is concerned, since interest rates have been fixed at a constant nominal level for many years, the only measure that the monetary authority has employed to influence this level is to launch political campaigns to urge households to maintain a higher level of balances in their saving deposit accounts.

As for cash withdrawal (equation (5)), the single most important factor was the sale of consumption goods to households (RT). Figures in Table 1.5 indicate that, prior to the economic reform, such sales plus sales of services and fees, together accounted, on average, for about 70 per cent to 80 per cent of the annual withdrawal of currency in circulation from the non-bank public. Again, the Chinese monetary authority was not able to exercise any control over these factors which depended primarily on the actual annual supply of consumer goods in any given year.

The lack of success in controlling the key factors in cash withdrawal and injection was relatively less significant in the context of the monetary authority's passive role in implementing the government's comprehensive fiscal and credit funds planning. Because currency in circulation was only one 'source' of funds for bank credits they in turn accounted for a small portion of the CFP before the reform (Table 1.1). In practice, the Chinese monetary authority has traditionally resorted to a simple rule in the actual planning for the growth of currency supply.[27] The rule is based on the Fisher's equation of exchange version of the quantity theory of money:

$$c = p + g - v$$

that is, the planned growth rate of currency in circulation (c) is the sum of the forecast growth rate in the general price level (p), planned real output growth rate (g) and change in money velocity (v). Usually the retail price index is used to represent general price change. In the actual planning process, however, the velocity factor is often dropped.[28] Therefore, currency growth is to accommodate the expected change in national output and prices. Indeed, Chinese

Table 1.4 Sources of annual cash injection* (percentage share)

Year	Wages and bonus WA	Agricultural procurement PR	Credit co-operatives RCJ	Saving deposit payout SJ	Administration management costs, rural units, individual business GE	Remittances and others ORJ
1953	25	24	5	5	5	36
1954	27	29	1	10	6	26
1955	29	29	2	12	7	22
1956	32	18	6	15	8	21
1957	35	15	11	13	7	20
1958	32	10	14	18	9	17
1959	30	11	12	16	8	17
1960	40	6	14	20	8	12
1961	45	7	16	15	6	11
1962	47	11	15	11	6	11
1963	46	15	14	neg	6	19
1964	46	15	14	neg	6.	19
1965	44	17	15	9	6	9
1966	43	17	16	9	6	9
1967	43	16	17	neg	6	18
1968	44	15	17	neg	6	17
1969	43	13	18	neg	6	20
1970	45	12	18	neg	6	18
1971	45	13	18	neg	6	9
1972	45	13	18	neg	6	7
1973	44	13	19	8	6	8
1974	44	12	20	9	7	9
1975	44	12	21	9	7	9
1976	44	11	21	9	7	8
1977	44	10	22	9	7	8
1978	46	9	22	10	6	8
1979	43	12	21	11	6	13
1980	42	13	22	11	6	10
1981	40	15	22	12	6	6
1982	37	16	24	13	6	5
1983	33	19	20	14	9	5
1984	32	18	20	15	10	6
1985	31	15	19	18	10	7
1986	32	15	18	19	10	6
1987	28	13	18	23	11	7
1988	24	11	16	30	11	9
1989	24	10	13	33	10	9
1990	24	10	13	33	10	10
1991	22	9	13	36	10	10

Source: *Almanac of China's Finance and Banking*, various issues
Note: * Injection into circulation from the state banking system

Table 1.5 Channels of cash withdrawal* (percentage share)

Year	Commodity sales RT	Services and fees FE	Savings deposits receipts SW	Credit Co-operatives RCW	Taxes, rural units, individual business TX	Remittances, receipts and others ORW
1953	67	3	6	4	5	14
1954	67	4	10	1	6	11
1955	68	5	12	1	5	9
1956	68	5	13	3	4	7
1957	66	6	13	6	3	6
1958	60	6	19	5	3	7
1959	56	6	17	9	2	11
1960	56	8	21	6	1	7
1961	57	12	15	6	1	9
1962	65	11	9	5	2	9
1963	69	9	neg	5	2	16
1964	69	8	neg	4	2	16
1965	69	8	10	4	1	8
1966	70	8	9	5	1	7
1967	72	7	neg	5	1	16
1968	71	8	neg	5	1	15
1969	70	7	neg	4	neg	18
1970	71	7	neg	4	neg	18
1971	70	8	neg	4	neg	18
1972	70	8	neg	4	neg	18
1973	71	8	9	4	1	8
1974	71	8	9	4	1	7
1975	72	8	9	4	1	7
1976	72	8	9	4	1	6
1977	72	8	9	4	1	6
1978	71	8	11	4	neg	6
1979	69	8	14	5	neg	5
1980	67	7	14	6	neg	5
1981	66	7	15	7	neg	5
1982	63	6	16	10	neg	5
1983	59	6	17	11	2	5
1984	56	6	20	11	2	5
1985	52	6	23	11	2	6
1986	50	6	25	11	2	6
1987	44	6	29	11	3	7
1988	41	5	34	9	3	8
1989	36	5	38	9	4	8
1990	33	6	40	10	4	8
1991	31	6	42	10	2	9

Source: Almanac of China's Finance and Banking, various issues

Note: * Withdrawal from circulation back to the state banking system

policy-makers have traditionally employed the above formula to bench-mark a target over which 'excessive' monetary (i.e. currency) growth is to be monitored and controlled.

On the one hand, this approach clearly shows how the Chinese monetary authority has quite incorrectly equated monetary control with the supply management of currency in circulation. No consideration is given to the changing money demand conditions as a result of the broader economic reform process. On the other hand, such an approach clearly provides a basis for a proactive accommodation of inflationary pressure, thus making the task of monetary management more difficult. The more significant factors, however, are the passive provision of bank credits to create transfer money, and the rigidity of planned state expenditure (E) which ultimately determine the volume of money flows.

4 FINANCIAL AND ECONOMIC REFORM: IMPACT ON MONETARY MANAGEMENT

Various forms and processes of decentralisation, deregulation and the extension and restoration of the market mechanism in all sectors of the Chinese economy have transformed and created new economic–social institutions and changed the behaviour of the economic agents which have rapidly increased in number. Despite these changes, the CFP framework remains very much the corner-stone of the Chinese government's macroeconomic and monetary management. The budget, the cash plan and the credit plan continue their dominance in the macroeconomic management of the country.[29] The key elements of the CFP framework remain in force. On the other hand, China's reform, apart from establishing the facade of a range of new financial institutions and assets commonly found in market economies, has also produced changes that further undermine the capacity of the monetary authority to carry out its monetary management function under the traditional framework. This section examines the empirical evidence on the financial and monetary developments during the reform period and will explain how they are hastening the erosion of the foundation of the unchanged framework for financial planning, and undermining effective monetary management and macroeconomic control.

The fiscal and enterprise reforms, notwithstanding their problems, have produced significant changes in the underlying elements on which China's approach to monetary management is based. Estimates in Table 1.1 clearly show that the importance of bank credits (L) in the overall CFP financing scheme has risen rapidly during the reform period (from 10 per cent in 1978 to 36 per cent in 1992).The share of the state budget funds (B) has at the same time declined from 90 per cent to 64 per cent. The distribution between the formal state budget revenues (BR) and the extrabudgetary revenues (XR) has also undergone an equally notable transformation. The share of the formal consolidated budget revenues (BR) fell by over one half from 68 per cent of the total CFP funding source in 1978 to 33 per cent in 1991. The relative contribution of the extra-budgetary revenues rose by half from 21 per cent to 31 per cent. The macroeconomic and monetary implications of these developments are certainly not trivial.

4.1 The state budget

The consolidated state budget set revenue and expenditure targets for both central and local governments. These plan targets applied to both the formal state budget and the extra-budgetary budget.

Consider first the formal state budget (BR). The Chinese government has been expressing serious concern about the declining share of its state budget revenues in relation to national income because the trend is believed to have impacted adversely on the government's capability to exercise macroeconomic management for achieving stability and income redistribution. It is not the purpose of this study to analyse fully the problems of China's fiscal reform. The more relevant analytical aspect here is to examine the Chinese government's continuing inability during the reform process to control effectively its budget targets, one of the few remaining areas where central command could be expected to be strong. Despite its diminishing importance in the CFP framework, the state budget (BR) still contributes almost one third of the amount of funds and is therefore a significant factor for the functioning of China's national financial planning and control.

However, the actual performance in the implementation of the state budget's planned expenditure and revenue targets has been poor. Although the state budget deficit (official or adjusted figure) has so far remained below 3 or 4 per cent of China's national output,[30] the problem with the budget process is much greater than the deficit figures suggest. Table 1.6 provides data on the

25

discrepancies between the annual plan targets and the realised outcomes in revenues and expenditure between 1979 and 1991. On the basis of the unadjusted official Chinese statistics,[31] these figures indicate a consistent record of significant failure in achieving the targets. Both revenue and expenditure targets have been regularly exceeded, usually with a wider discrepancy in the expenditure outcome. A *budget imbalance contribution index* is constructed to measure the relative magnitude of the net unplanned budget outcomes (all resulting in deficits except for 1985) as a proportion to the actual budget imbalance. The unplanned budget outcome is defined here as the difference between the expenditure discrepancy and revenue discrepancy (i.e. [*B-A*] in Table 1.6). The actual budget imbalance is the difference between the realised outcomes in budget expenditures and revenues. The index is presented in column *C* of Table 1.6. Given that an actual budget deficit was recorded for all years except 1985, the higher the positive value of the index means the greater the significance of the unplanned component.

Between 1979 and 1991, there were only three years (1982, 1987 and 1988) when the absolute levels of discrepancy between targets and outcomes in both expenditures and revenues were small, resulting in very low levels of the imbalance contribution index (−2, 0, −2 respectively). The negative value of the index in 1982 and 1988 is the result of a slightly greater discrepancy in revenues (column *A*) than in expenditures (column *B*). For other years, the index ranges from 20 per cent to 100 per cent for the nine years when there were official budget deficits, and to 239 per cent for the year 1985 when an official budget surplus was recorded. The factors responsible for the difficulties with the Chinese state budget are the subject of many recent studies[32] and will not be examined here. The lack of a tax base appropriate to the new economic conditions, the inefficiency and persistent losses in state enterprises, the growing amount of various forms of direct budget subsidies are well-known factors in China's budget difficulties. What is important to note in the context of China's financial planning and monetary management is that the declining fortune of the state revenues is being 'compensated' by the continuing fiscal dominance of the monetary regime. That really means the government has effectively shifted some of its fiscal burden to the banking sector and is therefore monetising its imbalances openly and in disguised forms. In addition, it should also be noted that the

Table 1.6 Discrepancy between planned and realised state budget revenues and expenditures

	Revenue discrepancy (100 million yuan) (A)	Expenditure discrepancy (100 million yuan) (B)	Budget imbalance contribution index (per cent) (C)
1979	(−)16.73	153.94	100
1980	22.33	69.83	37
1981	32.86	58.37	100
1982	19.47	18.81	(−)2
1983	16.99	30.45	31
1984	163.36	177.90	33
1985	331.40	279.79	239[1]
1986	118.79	189.34	100
1987	(−)10.39	(−)10.97	0
1988	73.52	72.07	(−)2
1989	91.07	109.40	20
1990	76.02	126.75	36
1991	167.78	246.99	40

Source: Chinese Finance Statistics 1950–1991, p. 184

Note: Minus signs in (*A*) and (*B*) indicate underfulfilled plan targets, positive numbers represent overfulfilled targets

(*A*) = Realised revenues − Planned revenues

(*B*) = Realised expenditures − Planned expenditures

$$(C) = \frac{(B) - (A)}{\text{Realised Budget Expenditures} - \text{Realised Budget Revenues}} \times 100\%$$

[1] A realised budget surplus, with an overfulfilled revenue target greater than an overshot expenditure target

changing role and structure of the state budget can affect the segmented monetary system and its control.

For instance, the provision of price subsidies and grants to loss-making state enterprises from the state budget funds is not just a problem of fiscal management. According to the author's estimates, China's total budget expenditures on price subsidies (9.4 billion yuan) and enterprise subsidies (6.6 billion yuan) was 16 billion yuan in 1978, accounting for about 12 per cent of the adjusted total budget expenditures.[33] Price subsidies and a significant proportion of enterprise subsidies would ultimately be channelled in the form of currency to the household sector.[34] By 1989, total budget expenditures on price subsidies (37 billion yuan) and enterprise subsidies (60 billion yuan) increased to about 97 billion yuan, representing 27 per cent of the adjusted total budget expenditures. Thus, while the total share of the state budget in funding the CFP has declined, it is at the same time facilitating a rising share of cash transactions within the expenditure flows. In a market economy with a unified monetary system, increasing cash transactions in this way need not present any problem. However, the monetary control based on the cash plan is not premissed upon this rising leakage from the non-cash transfer money circuit (through which much of the state budget flows) to the currency circuit. A related problem is that, in the increasingly difficult budgetary conditions, as the government often cannot honour its subsidies payments or pay them in time, the state banks are forced to provide credits, usually with additional funds from the central bank, to enable such payments to be effected.[35]

4.2 Extra-budgetary funds

The growth of the size of China's extra-budgetary funds, in absolute and relative terms, has alarmed some Chinese policy-makers who assert that the development harms the central government's capacity to achieve macroeconomic stability. It should however be recognised that in principle most extra-budgetary revenues and expenditures are still subject to a central plan, and that their growth can be regarded as an inevitable product of the process of decentralisation to local administration and enterprises. The primary concern of this chapter is not the economics of fiscal decentralisation in terms of optimal division of responsibilities and revenues among the multi-tier government structure, nor its implications for allocative efficiency and redistributive effects, but how the changing extra-budgetary flows during the reform period may impact on the financial and monetary system and its management.

Much criticism has been levelled against the growth of extra-budgetary funds because it is presumed that an ever-increasing share of the funds is being handed over to the more autonomous and free-spending state enterprises. Certainly since the reform state enterprises can exercise more control over their finance and are indeed active in seeking and creating new alternatives for funding their operation and investment activities, often without regard to repayment ability and risks. However, that does not mean that they are therefore the sole beneficiary of the expansion in extra-budgetary funds. On the basis of recently published statistics and information gained from interviews with Chinese researchers and officials, this author has estimated the amount and percentage shares of extra-budgetary revenues going to the local (provincial) fiscal authority, to the state enterprises (whether they are under direct central or local jurisdiction) and to the central and local ministries/departments that have supervisory responsibility over those enterprises. The results of the estimation are presented in Table 1.7.

Estimates in Table 1.7 show that, contrary to the common perception, the share of retained profit and incomes kept by state enterprises has actually been declining during the reform years, from the 27 to 30 per cent levels between 1982 and 1988 to only 17 per cent in 1991. Furthermore, the share of extra-budgetary funds going to central government ministries has in fact increased from 33 per cent in 1982 to 38 per cent in 1991. Indeed, for most of the years between 1982–91, the central ministries had a significantly higher share of the extra-budgetary funds than the local ministries. According to Chinese practices, extra-budgetary funds going to government ministries, especially those to central ministries, are supposedly placed under more stringent planning control. Therefore, the acknowledgement by the Chinese government that extra-budgetary funds are getting out of control reflects not an explosion of funds going to state enterprises but a real problem in binding both central and local ministries to extra-budgetary plan guidelines and targets. If the argument of the dysfunctional nexus between the local government and their 'own' enterprises[36] were valid, it is likely that the same argument would also apply to the central ministries and the enterprises they controlled in an environment where the agency-principal problem is increasingly pronounced and the interest of the state is poorly represented and protected.[37] Now that the enterprises are in fact found to be receiving a declining share of the extra-budgetary revenues, it can therefore be expected that, with the support of their respective central and local government ministry as mentors, they would and could lean on the state banking system to help fund their pursuit of fast expansion. The evidence on bank lending practices clearly attests to the problem. On the other hand, the funds thus provided may in a perverse way help the competitive development of state and particularly collective enterprises which have contributed much to China's marketisation and industrial growth. However, therein also lies a real problem. The inefficiency in fund allocation

Table 1.7 Distribution of extra-budgetary revenues (billion yuan)

Year	Local fiscal authority (A)	Local goverment – supervising departments and organisations (B)	Central government – supervising ministries and organisations (C)	Retained profits & income of state enterprises (central and local) (D)
1982	4.53	27.07	27.07	21.61
	(6%)	(33%)	(33%)	(27%)
1983	4.98	26.72	35.99	29.08
	(5%)	(28%)	(37%)	(30%)
1984	5.52	30.70	47.05	35.57
	(5%)	(26%)	(39%)	(30%)
1985	4.41	38.80	63.61	46.18
	(3%)	(25%)	(42%)	(30%)
1986	4.32	48.82	71.66	48.93
	(3%)	(28%)	(41%)	(28%)
1987	4.46	61.77	82.80	53.85
	(2%)	(30%)	(41%)	(27%)
1988	4.89	70.40	90.72	70.06
	(2%)	(30%)	(38%)	(30%)
1989	5.44	83.42	107.23	69.80
	(2%)	(31%)	(40%)	(26%)
1990	6.06	103.49	107.33	53.98
	(2%)	(38%)	(40%)	(20%)
1991	6.88	123.8	138.11	55.54
	(2%)	(38%)	(42%)	(17%)

Source: Column (A), Chinese Finance Statistics 1950–1991, p. 189; column (B), Chinese Finance Statistics 1950–1991, p. 187; 1993 Statistical Yearbook of China, p. 229; column (C), Chinese Finance Statistics 1950–1991, p. 193; 1993 Statistical Yearbook of China, p. 229; column (D), Chinese Finance Statistics 1950–1991, p. 301

Note: * Figures in brackets are percentage share of total annual extrabudgetary revenues

(B) = Total extra-budgetary revenues – (A) – (C) – (D)

and the duplication of unviable projects are the obvious adverse outcomes that are widely reported. The frequent loss of control over bank credits to enterprises, the growth in non-performing loans and worsening inter-enterprise arrears are the more apparent manifestations of that larger problem. It is also interesting to note that about 20 per cent of all extra-budgetary expenditures were spent on workers' benefits and bonuses, and administration,[38] most of which would be effected through cash transactions.

A seldom noticed and studied area is the balance of China's

Table 1.8 Extra-budgetary revenues and expenditures

	(A) Revenues (100 million yuan)	(B) Expenditures (100 million yuan)	(C) = (A) − (B) (100 million yuan)	(D) = (C) as % of official budget deficit
1982	802.74	734.53	68.21	232%
1983	967.68	875.81	91.87	211%
1984	1188.48	1114.74	73.74	166%
1985	1530.03	1375.03	155.00	717%*
1986	1737.31	1578.37	158.94	225%
1987	2028.80	1840.75	188.05	236%
1988	2360.77	2145.27	215.50	274%
1989	2658.83	2503.10	155.73	169%
1990	2708.64	2707.06	1.58	1%
1991	3243.30	3092.26	151.04	75%

Source: Chinese Finance Statistics 1950–1991, pp. 187, 210, 211; *1993 Statistical Yearbook of China*, p. 231

Note: * According to Chinese definintion, there was a budget surplus in 1985

extra-budgetary receipts and expenditures, which has been in surplus for all the reform period (Table 1.8). To place the size of the extra-budgetary balance in perspective, column *D* of the table shows the balance (surplus) as a percentage of the formal budget balance (official unadjusted figures, all deficits except for the year 1985). During the 1980s, the relative size of the extra-budgetary surplus ranged from an equivalent of 166 per cent of the formal budget deficit in 1984 to 274 per cent in 1988, and to 717 per cent of the formal budget surplus in 1985. The significance of these figures lies in the fact that all extra-budgetary surpluses are actually used by the central government although the use is not reported,[39] and that such surpluses are in absolute terms large enough to have wiped out the official deficits in the formal budget. In Chinese practice, the transfer of funds between the formal budget and the extra-budget scheme is allowed and common.[40] One can only speculate on the effect this may have on the behaviour of policy-makers responsible for the formal state budget, but the amount of extra-budgetary surplus available for use directly or indirectly in the formal budget is certainly not insignificant and cannot be ignored.

3.3 Bank credits and currency

An examination of the performance in the credit and cash plans in the CFP framework during the reform period provides an important key to understanding the problems in China's macroeconomic controls. The rapid increase in the importance of bank credits as a source of finance during the reform period (Table 1.1) now bestows on the partially reformed Chinese banking system a pivotal role in the country's monetary management. It is clear that, not entirely because of the banks' own failing, the fulfilment of that role remains a distant goal. For monetary control, the primary policy measures remain the cash plan and credit plan through which the level of bank lending is to be set by administrative orders.

As explained earlier, however, cash represents only one circuit of China's segmented monetary system. Thus, even if cash control were entirely successful, the effects on the country's monetary conditions will be partial. The credit plan in itself cannot really be considered as a policy instrument for the control of money supply as bank loans do not constitute any definition of money. In the traditional centrally planned system, however, it can be argued that money in this type of economic system is credit money created on demand by the extension of bank credits.[41] Accordingly, credit control is equivalent to monetary control and the use of a credit plan is therefore in principle justified. With the structural changes introduced during the reform period, that argument is further weakened. This section will attempt to provide some empirical evidence and explanations of these problems.

The level of bank lending has increased by several distinct leaps (usually followed by stagnant growth or credit contraction) during the reform period. As figures in Table 1.2 indicate, the level of new bank lending increased from 18 billion yuan in 1978 to 378 billion yuan in 1991, with rapid hikes in lending for the years 1980, 1984, 1986, 1989 and 1990. The stop-go and explosive cycles of bank lending are a clear indication that the Chinese monetary authorities have not been successful in exercising effective control over bank lending. Indeed, the plan target for bank credits has regularly been exceeded by a very large margin and is often revised upwards several times within a year.[42] The credit plan is clearly facing major difficulties in its implementation. The state banks have resorted to an increasing amount of loans from the central bank, which amounted on average to about half of the banks' total deposits for each year between 1985 and 1991. In other words, the central bank has been underwriting the credit expansion.

Under the CFP framework, the planned level of new bank credit (L) is based partly on the planned increase in total bank deposits (D). Since the start of the reform, as figures in Table 1.2 show, the importance of deposits as a source of credits, although fluctuating, has become predominant. However, the composition of total deposits has also gone through a significant transformation during the same period. Data in Table 1.3 indicate that the share of household deposits rose from 27 per cent of the total in 1978 to 54 per cent in 1991. The proportion of enterprise deposits correspondingly dropped from 73 per cent to 46 per cent. As far as monetary management is concerned, there are two major consequences from this change in the deposit mix.

First, compared to enterprise deposits which are normally subject to more restrictions in their uses, the level of household deposits is always more difficult to control administratively. Household deposits can be withdrawn quite freely and are determined by a variety of variables including the consumption and saving behaviour of individuals, the availability of alternative forms of financial assets, interest rates, income growth and other factors.[43] The monetary authorities could exercise little immediate influence over these variables other than marginally adjusting the highly regulated and sticky interest rates. Therefore, the level of risk and uncertainty in the planning of bank lending has risen with this structural change in bank deposits.

Second, it can be expected that for any given level of planned bank lending, there will be a correspondingly greater amount of transactions in the currency circuit than before the reform as the share of enterprise deposits has declined. However, the credit plan and the cash plan are still separately formulated and administered, thus presenting an additional complicating factor in the control of currency, which remains the focus of China's monetary policy.

When the PBC was established as the central bank of a new two-tier banking system in 1984, it was envisaged that the new central bank would, in concert with the gradual transition to a more market-oriented economy, develop indirect monetary policy instruments based on market force rather than direct command and centralised allocation. However, the conventional market-based policy instruments have so far failed to become a viable means for effective monetary and credit control.

After the credit explosion of the last quarter of 1984 (its first year as the designated central bank),[44] the PBC has since introduced and maintained a system of bank lending quotas. Annual quotas (with specified quotas for different types of loans) are given to the head office of each specialised bank, which breaks down the total amount and then allocates them to their local provincial branches for further subdivision. Despite some variation in its applications over the years and the introduction of other nominally market-based monetary policy instruments such as bank deposit reserve requirement, the quantitative bank credit quota system continues to be the primary means for credit control.

The problems with the credit quota system are many. The more obvious are its effects on entrenching the compartmentalised and regionalised mode of the flow of funds within a highly territorial approach by each local bank branch and each specialised bank. The problems of localisation and fragmentation of financial flows in the Chinese banking system are well known.[45] Local branches of the specialised banks readily succumb to political pressure from the local administration to extend bank credits. They routinely restrict the mobility of funds across administrative jurisdictions and even between different banks within the same region. This has certainly not contributed to the best utilisation and allocation of financial resources in the increasingly marketised economy.

The result is a fragmented banking system with no national market for the supply and demand of credits, adversely impacting on the mobilisation and utilisation of the country's financial resources. Given the compartmentalised credit flows, mismatchings of lending quotas and the capacity/demand for bank loans at the operational level often contribute to the unnecessary and unplanned expansion of total lending because unused quotas cannot be transferred from surplus branches to deficit branches that need to lend in excess of the given quotas. Clearly the capacity and efficiency of the banking system to mobilise and allocate financial resources are seriously impeded when both the quantity (the banks' major assets – loans) and price of finance (interest rates) are subject to quantitative controls.

In addition, there is also the tendency of the Chinese government, at all levels, to impose upon banks to fund designated priority areas or projects. Directed credits, or 'policy loans', coupled with all the other regulatory constraints, make it difficult for banks to even play the limited role of an arbiter in the imperfect process of credit rationing under a rigidly regulated interest rate regime. It has been estimated that over 90 per cent of the annual increase in bank credits for working capital in recent years resulted directly from government directions and intervention.[46] For 1991, there were 30 categories of directed bank loans, accounting for over 56 per cent of the annual bank lending.[47]

While some Chinese economists and Western observers may believe that such quantitative controls are necessary and effective in the current circumstances, the reality is that even such centralised means of monetary control did not work well. The continuing and frequent upward revisions in recent years of the largely ineffectual annual bank lending targets and quotas attest to this reality. Part of the difficulties stems from the institutions and behavioural responses derived from the continuing formal segmentation of cash and non-cash money, which was installed for an earlier economic system that has undergone much fundamental changes.

In summary, the effectiveness of the credit plan and the way it is being implemented are under unprecedented pressure. Certainly a major problem with credit control rests with the weakness of the central bank. It should also be noted that since the Chinese government permitted the development of alternative banking

Table 1.9 Cash plan implementation (100 million yuan)

	Plan Target of Increase in Currency in Circulation	Actual Increase in Currency in Circulation	Actual Increase as % of Target Increase
1984	80	262	328%
1985	100	195	195%
1986	200	230	115%
1987	230	236	103%
1988	200	680	340%
1989	400	210	53%
1990	400	300	75%
1991	500	533	107%
1992	600	1158	193%

Source: Xie Ping, 'The Three Major Problems in China's Monetary Policy', *Gaige (Reform)*, No. 3, 1993, p. 13

and' financial institutions from the mid 1980s, albeit on a limited scale, the share of bank credits extended by the state-owned banks has steadily declined from over 92 per cent of total bank loans in 1985 to 75 per cent in 1993.[48] Thus, as marketisation and financial development progress in China, the function of the credit plan is further eroded to render its intended objectives unachievable and its continued existence a hindrance in the development of viable monetary policy instruments for macroeconomic stability.

As for the cash plan, it is becoming even more problematic in its role as China's foremost monetary policy measure while the economic reform process continues. Consider first the data presented in Table 1.9 on the implementation performance of the cash plan in recent years. There is no doubt that, on the basis of those data, the cash plan has completely failed to target increases in the volume of currency in circulation. Even in the slow growth years of 1989 and 1990, the discrepancy between actual and plan target cash increase is over 50 per cent. For all other years, there has been an over 100 per cent margin of error, with the highest being 340 per cent in 1988 when the economy was generally regarded as being overheated. The factors influencing the poor result in cash plan implementation are not entirely dissimilar to those operating before the reform. However, there are also structural changes in cash injection and withdrawal and other systemic developments that have greatly exacerbated the problem.

In terms of cash injection, figures in Table 1.4 show that, after the economic reform, the composition of major channels through which currency is supplied from the state banking system to the economy has undergone significant changes. The share of cash injection through wage and bonus payments (*WA*) has declined sharply from 46 per cent in 1978 to 22 percent in 1991, whereas the share through saving deposit withdrawal (*SJ*) increased rapidly from 10 per cent to 36 per cent during the same period. On the cash withdrawal side, the changes in channels indicated by figures in Table 1.5 are similarly fundamental and reflect the same directional shift in the currency circuit. Cash withdrawal from the economy back to the state banking system through commodity sales (*RT*) was the predominant channel before the reform. Its share dropped from 71 per cent in 1978 to only 31 per cent in 1991, while the share through saving deposit receipts (*SW*) rose nearly four times from 11 per cent to 42 per cent.

The picture that emerges from the above figures is that the two major channels, wage payments and commodity sales, through which the Chinese government has traditionally (though not successfully) tried to exercise currency control have both lost their dominance. In their place, debits and credits in household saving deposits accounts are now the most important components of currency flows in and out of the state banking system. As discussed earlier in this chapter, the Chinese monetary authorities had little direct influence over the amount of wage payment and commodity sales. It is even more difficult to control the level of movements in the withdrawal and receipts of saving deposit accounts for the purpose of achieving the targets in the cash plan. Other things being equal, if the level of saving deposit is responsive to changes in interest rates, it is in principle possible to achieve a desired level of saving deposits by varying the rates of interest sufficiently in a timely fashion. However, even disregarding the still highly regulated and rigid interest rate regime under which Chinese banks have to operate, there are other strong factors at work that render the task of controlling currency flows in the cash plan context difficult to achieve.

One of these major factors is in fact the *de facto* breaking down of the institutional segmentation of cash and non-cash monetary circuits. Cash is extending into the previously prohibited realm of production and investment. Cash is no longer just the money used by households for consumption. At the same time there emerge expanding opportunites for transfer money to leak (be converted) into cash, partly to avoid the monitoring and supervision of the use of enterprise money by the banking system under the unchanged framework for monetary controls. As in many other economies, using cash is certainly also a convenient way of tax avoidance, which has become a real problem in China as well. Because of the wider money functions cash now commands, it has in reality gained the status of a 'good' money (compared with transfer money) and is preferred by market participants. Thus, in this reverse version of Gresham's Law, the use of the good money (cash) is actually expanding rapidly although this has not driven out the 'bad' money (transfer money) because of the latter's officially designated functions under the *de jure* continuation of the segmented monetary system.

There are extensive reports[49] that state enterprises are channelling their funds into the currency circuit by putting them in saving deposit accounts. This is done either through bogus personal accounts or their co-operative or collective enterprise offshoots. The net effect is a continuing rise in the volume of saving deposits and the amount of currency in the hands of households and enterprises. A major cause of the preference for cash is the fact that households and individual businesses cannot normally operate cheque accounts and must settle their transactions in cash. At the same time enterprises are still bound by highly restrictive regulations over the use of their transfer money. Therefore, as banks still play their role as a government administrative organ, the increase in money demand has concentrated primarily on cash. As a result the monetisation process in China is reflected perhaps more in the increase in cash use, in contrast to the conventional notion of monetisation in which barter exchanges are replaced by the use of money and spread of commercial banks.

There are in addition a number of developments that contribute to the expanding use of cash. For instance, the capacity to raise household cash income is now no longer limited to the state budgetary process. With the reform measures, more enterprises, state and collective-owned, have sufficient autonomy to effect discretionary power to raise household income in significant ways. This has resulted in a rapid increase in household income and in cash supply. The fast growing non-state enterprises, which accounted for just over half of the country's industrial output value in 1992,[50] often operate in cash as the state banking system focuses its services on the needs of state enterprises.[51]

The non-state enterprises must operate profitably in a highly competitive environment to survive. Even many state-owned enterprises, despite the institutional constraints imposed on them, are detected to behave competitively to maximise profit.[52] A related development is the corporatisation of an increasing number of state enterprises, in which many have set up separate corporate entities that operate autonomously in the competitive markets. The market, therefore, instead of the plan, is becoming the more important allocative mechanism in practice. Hence, a *raison d'être* for the separate use of transfer money as a tool of the centralised system of material balancing is no longer there.

In the rural area, the reform has resulted in *de facto* privatisation of most sectors of economic activity. As a result, the sheer number of economic agents and the amount of monetary transactions have increased many times. Farmers can now sell their products directly to households in cities. More significantly, the new market exchange relationship between the urban and rural sector is now driven strongly by the growth of rural township and village factories. A significant proportion of the population has moved into the non-agricultural sector. This development certainly promotes monetisation and the breaking down of the artificial separation of the two monetary circuits. Households in the cities are allowed to operate private enterprise business so that they are now participants in the investment process and in the producer-goods market.

Accompanying the changes in the real economic sectors, a new and independent circuit in currency flow has appeared. This part of cash circulates directly among sellers and buyers. The informal financial sector plays an important intermediary role: cash no longer passes only through the state banks. This new circuit is termed by Chinese economists as 'circulation outside the "body"' (*tiwai xunhuan*). Not unlike the initial stage of the development of the Eurocurrency markets, the emergence of the new circuit in China is a market response to bank restrictions and has the ability to create money. Although it is not possible to estimate here the real magnitude of this outside cash circuit, its existence clearly does not enhance the implementation of the cash plan.

The increase in household income, the growth of rural industries and decollectivisation, the emergence of private business and the expansion of markets, have all raised money demand, particularly demand for cash. In addition, the continuing inability of households and private businesses to operate cheque accounts, and the fact that the entire fund transfer and settlement mechanism among financial institutions and economic agents remains outdated, inefficient and open to abuse, have combined to exert tremendous pressure on the country's payments system. Meanwhile, however, the banking system in China has not given up its function as an administrative organ for government interventions in the economy. This clearly is not conducive to meeting the new demands for financial development and monetisation.

Given the continuing existence of the CFP framework, improving the effectiveness of controls over bank credits and currency flows should have been given greater emphasis in China's monetary management during the reform. This is particularly important as there will be an increasing leakage between the two previously separate circuits of cash and transfer money flow. Unfortunately, the current outdated monetary management framework is shown to be incapable of maintaining effective controls over these flows.

4.4 The banking system

Since its establishment in 1984, China's two-tier banking system has certainly facilitated some reform policy measures but has at the same time been made to operate in ways that often run contrary to the objectives of a well-functioning banking system and not in the interest of economic reform and macroeconomic management. The explanations for this outcome can be found in the banking sector's operational mechanism and policy environment mandated by the Chinese government's pursuit of various economic and political goals. Although the PBC now nominally functions as a central bank, the specialised banks and the PBC are in practice integral parts of a complex but often contradictory contraption of banking relations to serve passively the government's needs through the increasingly ineffectual CFP mechanism. This section will present a brief overview of the central bank and the state banks.

Relying mainly on predetermined quantitative controls as monetary policy instruments, the PBC is really continuing its traditional functions in a vastly different economic and financial environment. The PBC's major regulatory tools are still the credit plan and cash plan despite their increasingly apparent inadequacy. On the one hand, transfer money is no longer limited to the producer-goods sectors but its creation has been out of control for nearly the whole reform period. On the other hand, the use of lending quotas as a last resort has further severed the link between deposits and loans so that the token bank reserve system cannot be made to operate to restrain bank lending.

There is no doubt that the Chinese monetary authorities will have increasingly to employ market-based policy instruments in order to attain their macroeconomic and monetary goals as the economy continues its transition to dismantle centralised allocation of resources and restore the functions of the market in the economy. Some economists inside and outside the Chinese government have regarded the inadequate number of monetary policy instruments as a main reason for PBC's ineffectual monetary and credit controls. However, the lack of central bank independence, the growth and social policy mandates imposed by the government and the internal organisational problems of the PBC itself are no less important in determining the actual outcomes in its monetary management.

As far as the PBC is concerned, there seems to be ample evidence to suggest that serving the Chinese government's economic growth policy has priority over maintaining monetary stability. This growth-oriented policy essentially means that the Chinese government will not tolerate economic and financial adjustments that require prolonged static growth that might threaten to bring about large-scale retrenchment and open unemployment. The banking system is therefore required to ensure funding to maintain the survival of state enterprises and to provide loans to designated projects or enterprises under the government's industry policy.

More importantly, the PBC has allowed and facilitated the banking sector's overall continuing credit expansion in support of the unprofitable and inefficient state-owned enterprise system and the deficit spending at all levels of government. This soft approach to managing bank credit expansion is the result of the PBC having a subordinate position in the Chinese government. Suggestions that the enterprise budget constraint be made 'hard' at the firm level without transforming the banking system and severing the link between the banks and the financial planning framework are therefore unlikely to work in the long run.

The conclusion that can be drawn is that, under the CFP framework and economic mandates of the Chinese government, the central bank is not in a position to pursue active and effective policies for monetary stability. Its present role is not significantly different in essence from its past and appears to be still passive and subordinate. It has so far not been able to employ conventional market-based policy instruments to influence and adjust monetary conditions in the economy. The administrative controls available to the PBC, the credit and cash plans, are not enforceable for long in the face of demands for growth and survival of the massive and inefficient (though declining) state-owned enterprise sector.

China's four specialised banks are the dominant financial institutions in the country. These banks were originally set up to give effect to the transition from a centralised financial system to a more decentralised and market-oriented one. Each bank was to serve a designated sector or type of transaction, although the demarcation has quickly become blurred as specialised banks actively compete for business. Apart from the usual problems associated with credit rationing under regulated interest rates, the

Chinese banks are handicapped because they are also given quotas and targets under the current credit plan for most types of lending.

To improve the performance of the specialised banks to meet the demand of China's economic reform requires changes in the central bank's monetary management approach and ultimately a genuine rethinking of the financing of the public sector and the state-owned enterprises. In other words, *the CFP framework with its associated institutions has to be abandoned.* In the immediate term, apart from strengthening the financial and accounting discipline of the banks themselves, specialised bank performance can be improved by reducing and eliminating all lending activities that are really a disguised form of monetising state budget imbalance. That means that using directed loans as a roundabout and disguised means of monetising the imbalances in government spending should be discontinued. If the targeted projects or enterprises are considered to be socially or politically desirable, the Chinese government will have to either subsidise them directly or set up separate institutions (such as development banks) to supply them with specially funded capital. The development of capital markets will also be needed.[53] Furthermore, instead of being preoccupied with regulatory quantitative controls over credit quota allocation and interest rates, the central bank should devote more efforts to creating a competitive and secure environment for the development of commercial banks and non-bank financial institutions, and a system of monitoring, evaluating and prudential supervision, not just over the quantity but also the quality of the assets and liabilities of financial institutions.

It is interesting to note that, despite all the regulatory restrictions, the state banking system (including the PBC, which still carries out lending to enterprises and units), with its sheer business volume, has become a *major source of budget revenue* during a period when state enterprises are declining as a revenue contributor. This author has estimated that the banking system contributed about one quarter to the 'tax and profit revenue' category of the Chinese state (consolidated) budget in 1989.[54] Therefore, it can be expected that there will be a vested interest from the Ministry of Finance and other government departments that depend on state budget funds to see that this revenue source is not endangered. The implication is that increasing profit from continuing bank credit expansion may not be inconsistent with the short-term interest of many powerful ministries. In the absence of relevant information and data, it is not possible to determine whether the bank profits are genuine and represent a real contribution to the budget. Nevertheless, as state industrial enterprises could make accounting profit under a distorted price system and contribute revenue to the budget, it is conceivable that banks can also do the same.

5 CONCLUSION

As China's economic reform proceeds, prices are becoming less regulated and rigid and market competition is being re-introduced in many spheres of economic activity. Monetary management in China, however, still remains in the realm of central planning and is held hostage to the government's financial needs. The essential elements of the traditional financial planning mechanism, as represented in the CFP model in this study, have not been abandoned in the face of significant changes in the country's economic and financial systems. The supply-oriented and quota-based monetary stand, as expressed in the cash and credit plans, has become increasingly untenable with the process of monetisation and financial reform.

The ultimate cause of many of the problems in China's monetary management can be traced back to the maintenance of its CFP framework supported by a passive banking system at a time when marketisation and monetisation have changed the premisses of such a mechanism. The financial reform in China, despite the introduction of some new institutions and instruments, has not yet created the conditions necessary for more effective monetary management based on market demand and supply.

The reform of China's financial system has reached a stage when rethinking on how best to continue the process becomes vital to its success. While both the bank and non-bank financial sectors have experienced rapid changes and growth in recent years, there are also major problems and conflicts that need to be resolved before the financial system can perform its basic functions efficiently. Some of the issues will involve fundamental reappraisal of the Chinese government's economic and political goals. For instance, the role of the government at various levels, the financing of the public sector and the provision of public goods and welfare in the economy, and the form and extent of the ownership of state enterprises, are basic questions to be urgently addressed to ensure that the economic reform process can be sustained without incurring the high costs associated with the recent disruptions and instability.

There are also issues that are directly linked to the functioning of the financial system and can generally be tackled from within the system. These relate to how efficient a role the financial system can play in financial resource mobilisation and allocation, in providing an effective mechanism and environment for monetary management, and in facilitating and promoting systemic changes in other areas of the economy to enhance the economic reform and development process.

It is now commonly accepted that economic development benefits greatly from a process of financial development. A well functioning and efficient financial system is the key factor in a country's financial development. China's gradual transition to a more market-oriented and open economic system has given rise to a new and significantly expanded role for money and finance in all spheres of economic activities. Whereas the traditional financial development theories have placed emphasis on the liberalisation and deregulation of interest rates, China's financial reform will require appropriate institution-building as well as reducing government's direct intervention in the flows of financial resources.

The reform of China's financial system has primarily been carried out as a vehicle for achieving other economic reform objectives. In its static role, China's financial reform will need to improve its effectiveness and efficiency in mobilisation and allocation of financial resources for both the traditional state-owned industries and the increasingly more important and vibrant non-state sector. At the same time, the reform of the financial system should also have a dynamic and developmental role in the economy by inducing positive changes and reforms in other areas of the economy such as the state budget and enterprise reforms. A major function in this context is the provision of an appropriate mechanism and environment for market competition, risk taking and financial disciplines that satisfy the demands of the market-oriented economic reform and through which macroeconomic and monetary management can be carried out effectively.

At the microeconomic level, reforming the financial system can help enhance factor and product mobility, market development, price and ownership reform. Because the Chinese economic system before the reform had restricted severely the role of finance

44

and retarded the development of a financial system, and since the Chinese government has consistently maintained that it does not intend to withdraw all regulations and interventions in the economy, financial reform will need to create the right kind and number of institutions to improve the functioning of both the fledgling market and the public sector, and not just reduce the role of government.

The question now is what can be done to improve the performance of the financial system so that economic growth can be sustained, and the market-oriented reform proceed with stability. It is clear that China will need to unify its money by ending the segmentation of cash and transfer money, and abandon the traditional framework of financial planning and management.

There has certainly been no lack of suggestions from both Chinese and Western observers to reform the Chinese banking system. For instance, a recent suggestion by McKinnon (1992) was to restrict bank credits to traditional state enterprises and to exclude 'liberalised enterprises' from bank credit eligibility at the first stage of transition. McKinnon's aim was to 'harden' the budget constraint on enterprises. However, notwithstanding the problems arising from the fungibility of finance, the suggested scheme is unlikely to work in the present phase of Chinese economic reform because the distinction between traditional enterprises and 'liberalised' enterprises is no longer clear. More importantly, as noted earlier, if the banking system were to be left fundamentally unchanged and its role in monetising the state budget imbalance (whether in open or disguised forms) were not discontinued, then the hardening of the state enterprise budget will be impossible and not significant in its effect.

Apart from the need for a new model of public finance, including a wider and more viable tax base and revenue-sharing arrangements, there are a number of reform options for the monetary system that can be considered. First, the official segmentation of the cash and non-cash money circuit must be ended. Individuals and enterprises should all be allowed to use cash for transactions and all should be allowed to operate cheque accounts. The traditional financial planning model should be abandoned and the banking system's link to state finance severed. Disguised monetisation of the state's income and expenditure imbalance through direct and indirect bank borrowings should cease.

Second, the banking system must improve its performance as a financial system and at the same time assist the reform in public finance and enterprise reform. It is paramount that the commercial banks be allowed to pursue their own market objectives within a suitably reconstituted prudential framework of bank regulations. In this context, there are merits in allowing the reorganisation of each of the four major specialised banks to break up and to merge with one another on a voluntary and commercial basis. For instance, the provincial branches of the ICBC and ABC in a particular province (or region) may decide to merge to form a new regional bank. Such reorganisations are consistent with the reality of market development and the strong social and political interests that prevail at this stage of China's development.

Furthermore, such new regional banks should be allowed if prudential conditions are met to perform the functions of a 'main bank' in the Japanese mode, where banks hold equity in enterprises and play a vital role in their corporate governance, so that genuine enterprise reform can be facilitated and implemented more extensively and more effectively. It can be expected that positive competition among banks and banking practices that enhance competition in other sectors will be intensified. These new banks will bring an important element of stability to China's fledgling stock-markets as cross-shareholding spreads. The passive accommodating nature of the Chinese banking system can thus be corrected.

As for the entry of private banks and foreign banks, there is a case for their full operation, including local currency business, particularly in the economically more advanced regions. There is an increasing demand for an expanding range of bank services. Such banks can better service these new markets by providing quality products with new technology and management expertise. Their participation will facilitate the ending of monetary segmentation through their contribution to the development of a modern national payments system in terms of technology, equipment and management. On the basis of recent experience in Australia, for instance, most foreign banks are unlikely to become dominant provided that the domestic banks are permitted to operate in all areas. Thus, concerns about the threat to the survival of domestic banks may be unjustified.

It is clear that both the central bank and the specialised banks will need to attain a much higher degree of independence and autonomy, with the corresponding financial responsibility and discipline, before China's financial system can perform all its expected microeconomic and macroeconomic functions efficiently. Such a move will inevitably require adjustment in the areas of fiscal and enterprise finance. However, there still remains vast scope for initiatives by the Chinese central bank and specialised banks to improve their operations and management of the country's money and credit flows without all the prerequisites of systemic changes in other areas. The interest rate structure, the mechanism for credit volume control, deposit reserve requirement and central bank lending to the specialised banks can be improved quickly to produce positive results. With the unification of the segmented monies and the transformation of the banking system, what is needed is a well co-ordinated programme of policy actions that will increase efficiency and market discipline on the basis of a more transparent and stable regulatory framework.

The growth of the non-state sector and the decentralisation at the regional and enterprise level offer new demand and exert pressure on further reform of the financial system. The banking system has responded passively to this new challenge, whereas the non-bank financial sector has been actively supporting, and indeed thrived on, this fast-developing product of the economic reform process. The issues of intra- and inter-sector competition and prudential supervision have to be addressed by the Chinese monetary authorities. The recent experiments with market-based trading of some government bonds and the establishment of stock-markets demonstrate the possibilities and benefits that can be attained when new and well-conceived reform measures are introduced to the financial system.

Although the Chinese government has retained a complex system of foreign exchange controls that has isolated the domestic financial system from the internationalisation of the financial markets, the rising openness of the Chinese economy means that such controls will become more and more inconsistent and incompatible with the economic development process. Therefore, the reform of the Chinese financial system will also have to make necessary adjustments in its external financial relations in view of such trends. Despite the constant disruptions, problems and uncertainties, the broad direction of China's economic reform has been maintained. The reform has made discernable progress and produced new opportunities and benefits. The financial system can and should be further transformed so that it can assist the economic reform and development process and reduce the likelihood and magnitude of economic instability.

Notes

1 Estimates of saving shares by Xie Ping, 'An Analysis of Personal Saving Behaviour in China-Part 1', *Jinrong Yanjiu (Financial Research)*, No. 8, 1993, p. 25

2 *People's Bank of China Annual Report 1992*

3 Suggestion by R. I. McKinnon, 'Financial Control in the Transition from Classical Socialism to a Market Economy', *Journal of Economic Perspectives*, Vol. 5, No. 4, 1991, pp. 107–122, and *The Order of Economic Liberalization: Financial Control in the Transition to a Market Economy* (Baltimore: Johns Hopkins University Press, 1992). There is no disagreement over McKinnon's and others' emphasis on establishing a wider and more viable tax base and achieving macroeconomic stability.

4 See, for example, C. H. Chai, 'Domestic Money and Banking Reform in China', *Hong Kong Economic Papers*, No. 14, 1981, pp. 37–52; W. Byrd, *China's Financial System – The Changing Role of the Banks* (Boulder, Col.: Westview Press, 1983); O. K. Tam , 'China's Banking Reform', *The World Economy*, December 1986; L. De Wulf and D. Goldsbrough, 'The Evolving Role of Monetary Policy in China', *IMF Staff Papers*, Vol. 33, No. 2, June 1986; G. Peebles, *Money in the People's Republic of China* (Sydney: Allen & Unwin, 1991); McKinnon (1992)

5 For more recent works on this subject that are more oriented towards developing and socialist economies see, for example, M. J. Fry, *Money, Interest, and Banking in Economic Development* (Baltimore: The Johns Hopkins University Press, 1988); C. Kessides *et al.* (eds), *Financial Reform in Socialist Economies* (Washington DC: World Bank, 1989); McKinnon (1992).

6 For instance, McKinnon (1992, pp. 3–4 and 120–123) suggested that China lost controls over the country's monetary conditions after its financial liberalisation, and that China undertook a premature banking decentralisation that led to uncontrolled credit flows.

7 For instance, Stiglitz raised the important question of whether the new banking system in the post-socialist East European economies should be involved in or barred from participating in production enterprises. Others, such as McKinnon, have advocated that banks should not provide credits to newly liberalised enterprises at the initial stage of reform. See J. E. Stiglitz (1992), 'The Design of Financial System for the Newly Emerging Democracies of Eastern Europe', in C. Clague and G. C. Rausser (eds), *The Emergence of Market Economies in Eastern Europe* (Cambridge, Mass.: Basil Blackwell), pp. 161–184.

8 For instance, McKinnon was rightly alerted to the assumption of a unified monetary system in the non-standard analysis of Polish repressed inflation with general price-wage control but ignored the issue and its implications in his discussion of China. R. McKinnon (1993) 'Gradual versus Rapid Liberalization in Socialist Economies: The

Problem of Macroeconomic Control', *Proceedings of the World Bank Annual Conference on Development Economics 1993*, pp. 63–94.

9 The most conspicuous examples are the various 'wool wars' and 'aluminium wars' that were the product of regional barriers set up by local governments to maximise local income at any cost. The less transparent but no less significant example is the barriers to the mobility of money and finance between different localities. For discussion of these topics, see A. Watson and C. Findlay, 'Who Won The "Wool War"?', *The China Quarterly*, No. 118, June 1989; O. K. Tam, 'The Development of China's Financial System', *Australian Journal of Chinese Affairs*, No. 17, January 1987.

10 For more discussions of the analytical implications of this dual but segmented money system in China, see, O. K. Tam (1992), 'Model of Chinese Monetary Management', *Department of Economics and Management Working Paper No. 1*, 1992, University of New South Wales; B. X. Huang, *An Analysis of Money Control in China*, (unpublished Ph.D. dissertation, University of New South Wales, Canberra, 1993).

11 For general discussion of the quantity theory, see, D. Laidler (1991), 'The Quantity Theory is Everywhere Controversial – Why?', *Economic Record*, Vol. 67, No. 199, December, pp. 289–306; for a view of its relevance to China, see G. Peebles (1992), 'Why the Quantity Theory of Money is Not Applicable to China, Together with a Tested Theory That Is', *Cambridge Journal of Economics*, 16, pp. 23–42.

12 For a survey of these issues, see, for example, S. M. Goldfeld and D. E. Sichel, 'The Demand for Money' in B. M. Friedman and F. H. Hahn (eds), *Handbook of Monetary Economics, Volume 1* (Amsterdam: North-Holland, 1990), pp. 299–356; J. L. Swofford and G. A. Whitney, 'The Composition and Construction of Monetary Aggregates', *Economic Inquiry*, October 1991, pp. 752–761.

13 See G. Chow, 'Money and Price Level Determination in China', *Journal of Comparative Economics*, Vol. 11, 1987; A. Feltenstein and Z. Farhadian, 'Fiscal Policy, Monetary Targets and the Price Level in a Centrally Planned Economy: an Application to the Case of China', *Journal of Money, Credit and Banking*, Vol. 19, 1987, pp. 137–156; A. Feltenstein, D. Lebor and S. van Wijnbergen, 'Savings, Commodity Market Rationing, and the Real Rate of Interest in China', *Journal of Money, Credit and Banking*, Vol. 22, No. 2, May 1990, pp. 252–255; G. Yi, 'The Monetisation Process in China During the Economic Reform', *China Economic Review*, Vol. 2, No. 1, 1991, pp. 75–95; R. W. Hafer and A. M. Kutan, 'Further Evidence on Money, Output and Prices in China', *Journal of Comparative Economics*, Vol. 17, 1993, pp. 701–709.

14 Most of the works mentioned in the preceding note are econometric models based on variants of the quantity theory. A small number of studies have examined various aspects of the institutions and mechanisms of money supply and demand. See, for example, A. Santorum, 'The Control of Money Supply in Developing Countries: China, 1949–1988', *ODI Working Paper 29*, 1989; Peebles (1991); Tam (1992); Huang (1993).

15 However, even in the well established literature on money demand

and supply in industrialised market economies, choices of an explicit measure of money are not always clear-cut. Uniform measure for money is not common, and the choice is often dictated by data availability. Indeed, problems with the definition of monetary aggregates are a continuing concern. See, for example, W. A. Barnett, 'The Optimal Level of Monetary Aggregation', *Journal of Money, Credit and Banking*, November 1982, part 2, pp. 687–710; and J. L. Swofford and G. Whitney, 'The Composition and Construction of Monetary Aggregates', *Economic Inquiry*, Vol. XXIX, October 1991, pp. 752–761.

16 It should be noted that only an insignificant amount of the enterprise deposits in such an account could in fact be drawn through the use of a cheque. Most deposit and withdrawal transactions were effected through book entries carried out and monitored by the bank.

17 China's monetary system was patterned on the Soviet model. In that system, 'when the Gosbank makes a loan to an enterprise, it does not draw upon the population's savings deposits or funds in enterprise/organisations' current accounts, it actually creates new money to make that loan'. (S. M. Ignatev, 'The Banking System: Paths of Reform', *Problems of Economics*, Vol. 32, No. 1, May 1989, pp. 89–104.) Transfer money would have fitted in comfortably with Wicksell's 'pure credit economy' in which all exchange was mediated by the transfer of bank deposits (Laidler 1991, p. 296).

18 The author has performed econometric tests of China's money velocity behaviour on the basis of the conventional definition of M_1 and M_2, using two approaches: (1) a 'standard' benchmark equation; (2) Bordo and Jonung's institutional approach. Tests using these approaches on Chinese data for the period 1950–90 are performed and the results are available from the author. Neither approach is found to produce satisfactory results. See M. D. Bordo and L. Jonung, *The Long Run Behaviour of the Velocity of Circulation* (Cambridge: Cambrige University Press, 1987) and 'The Long Run Behaviour of Velocity: the Institutional Approach Revisited', *Journal of Policy Modelling*, Vol. 12, No. 2, pp. 165–197.

19 For a quantitative study of the effects of the money segmentation on money demand, see, O. K. Tam and B. X. Huang, *Money Velocity Behaviour in China* (Mimeo, Department of Economics and Management, University of New South Wales, Canberra, 1993).

20 The Chinese refer to the framework as *Zhonghe Caizheng Xindai Zijin Pingheng*. For discussion of the general principles of the framework, see Xu Yi and Chen Bao-Sen, *Cai Zheng Xue* (*The Theory of Public Finance*) (Beijing: Chinese Fiscal and Economics Press, 1984), pp. 315–336.

21 De Wulf and Goldsbrough (1986) mentioned the existence of a financial plan involving the budget, credit plan and cash plan but then stated that 'the operation of monetary policy in this system could therefore best be described as the set of rules and practices adopted to implement the credit and cash plans', thus ignoring the interrelationship and structure of the financial plan and the fact that under a system where government deficits were fully monetised, there cannot be separate monetary and fiscal policies.

22 See note 17.

23 Researchers who have come to this conclusion from various approaches include, for example, Feltenstein and Farhadian (1987), R. Portes and A. Santorum, 'Money and the Consumption Goods Market in China', *Journal of Comparative Economics*, Vol. 11, September 1987, pp. 345–371; Santorum (1989); B. X. Huang, 'Huobi gongqiu fenxi' ('An Analysis of The Supply and Demand For Money'), ch. 6 in Zhang F. (ed.), *Zhongguo Hongguan Jingji Jiegou yu Zhengce (The Structure and Policy of China's Macroeconomy)* (Beijing: Chinese Finance and Economics Press, 1988), pp. 187–224; Tam (1992).

24 Under Chinese central planning, all state expenditures were to be funded either by budget revenues or bank credits and the principle that the two sources should be balanced separately and jointly had always been held up as the unique superiority of socialist economic management. For detailed description and discussion of the topic, see Li C. R., *Caizheng Xindai yu Guomin Jingjide Zhonghe Pingheng (Budget, Credits, and the Integrated Balance of the National Economy)* (Beijing: People's Press, 1982); Budget Division, Ministry of Finance, *Guojia Yusuanxue (The State Budget)*(Beijing: Chinese Fiscal and Economics Press, 1986); Deng Z. J., *Caizheng yu Xindai (Budget and Credit)* (Beijing: Chinese Finance and Economc Press, 1986); Tian Y. N. *et. al.*, *Lun Zhongguo Caizheng Tizhi Gaige yu Hongguan Tiaokong (On China's Fiscal Reform and Macroeconomic Control and Adjustment)* (Beijing: Chinese Finance and Economics Press, 1988).

25 In the pre-reform period, the banking system was based on the monobanking system, with the People's Bank of China performing both central bank and commercial bank activities.

26 See Chu Yangfa *et al.* (eds), *Yinhang Xindai Guanlixue (Bank Credit Management Study)* (Beijing: Chinese Finance and Economics Press, 1985), pp. 28–29; Wang Haibo (ed.), *Studies of Sectoral Economic Efficiency in the Chinese Economy* (in Chinese) (Beijing: Economic Management Press, 1990), pp. 388–389.

27 That rule (c = p + g) has in fact been applied continuously during the reform period. See Ma Hong and Sun Shangqing (eds), *Economic Situation and Prospects of China 1989–1990* (in Chinese) (Beijing: Zhongguo Fazhan Chubanshe, 1990), pp. 265–266.

28 Ma Hong and Sun Shangqign (eds), *Economic Situation and Prospects of China 1990–1991* (Beijing: Zhongguo Fazhan Chubanshe, 1991); Xie Ping, 'The Three Main Problems of Our Country's Monetary Policy', *Gai Ge (Reform)*, No.3, 1993, p. 12.

29 See for example, Li Gui-Xian, 'Speech to National Conference of Bank Branch Directors', *Jinrong Shibao (Financial Daily)*, 21 January 1993; Ma and Sun (1991).

30 *China Financial Statistics (1950–1991)*; Tam (1990).

31 Although it is well known that there are anomolies in the official Chinese budget data because of the treatment of government borrowings as budget income and government subsidies as negative revenues, it is not feasible to examine the discrepancies between plan targets and the actual budget outcomes by using adjusted

figures (to conform to international convention) as all targets were formulated according to official definitions.

32 See for example, Tian Y. N., Xiang H. C. and Zhu F. L., *Lun Zhongguo Caizheng Gaige yu Hongguan Tiao Kong* (*On China's Fiscal System Reform and Macro Adjustment*) (Beijing: Chinese Fiscal and Economic Press, 1988); K. Huang-Hsiao, *The Government Budget and Fiscal Policy in Mainland China* (Taipei: Chung-Hua Institution for Economic Research, 1989); The World Bank, *China: Revenue Mobilization and Tax Policy* (Washington, DC: The World Bank, 1989); C. P. W. Wong, 'Fiscal Reform and Local Industrialization', *Modern China*, Vol. 18, No. 2, April 1992, pp. 197–227; M. Oksenberg and J. Tong, 'The Evolution of Central–Provincial Fiscal Relations in China, 1971–1984: The Formal System', *The China Quarterly*, No. 125, March 1991, pp. 1–32; O. K. Tam and K. Forster, 'Chinese Fiscal Reform – Editors' Introduction', *Chinese Economic Studies*, Vol. 24., Nos 1 & 2, fall and winter 1990.

33 While the construction of the imbalance index in Table 1.6 can only be made on the basis of official unadjusted budget figures because all budget plan targets are similarly defined, the estimation of the relative importance of subsidies in budget expenditures must be based on adjusted budget figures due to their treatment in official data as negative revenues. The adjusted budget expenditures are equal to the sum of the official budget expenditure plus total price and enterprise subsidies minus repayment of public debts. Sources of information for the estimation are: *Chinese Statistical Yearbook*, various issues; Fan Wei-Zhong and Wu Jia-Jun, *Gongye Qiye Kuisun Diaocha Yanjiu* (*An Investigative Survey and Study of China's Loss-Making Enterprises*) (Beijing: Economic Management Press, 1989); State Statistical Bureau.

34 It is commonly acknowledged that enterprises often channel their subsidies to pay wage rises, bonus and other expenditure items on consumption for which cash money would be used. There are certainly strong incentives and the conditions for engaging in such behaviour. See Li Yang, 'An Economic Analysis of Enterprise Subsidies', *Jingji Yanjiu* (*Economic Research*), No. 1, 1990, pp. 72–78; Fan and Wu (1989).

35 *Jingrong Yanjiu* (*Financial Research*), No. 2, 1992, p. 26.

36 O. K. Tam, *Fiscal Policy Issues In China*, paper presented at the Institute of East Asian Studies, University of California, Berkeley, October 1990; C. P. W. Wong, 'Fiscal Reform and Local Industrialization', *Modern China*, Vol. 18, No. 2, 1992.

37 For discussion of this problem see O. K. Tam, 'Large and Medium-size State Enterprise Performance under China's Fiscal Reform', in Y. Y. Kueh (ed.) (forthcoming), *Industrial Transformation under China's Fiscal and Monetary Reform* (Oxford University Press); O. K. Tam, 'Corporate Governance and China's Listed Companies', *Corporate Governance: An International Review*, Vol. 3, No. 1, 1995, pp. 21–29.

38 *Chinese Finance Statistics 1950–1991*, pp. 210–211.

39 Division of Fiscal and Taxation Reform, Ministry of Finance, *Caishui*

Gaige Shinian (*Ten Years of Fiscal and Tax Reform*) (Beijing: Chinese Fiscal and Economics Press, 1989), p. 331.

40 Yang Z. M. and Fan H. S., *Difang Caizheng Guanli* (*Local Government Financial Management*) (Beijing: Chinese Fiscal and Economics Press, 1990), pp. 169–171.

41 For full discussion of the concept of credit money, see, B. J. Moore, *Horizontalists and Verticalists: The Macroeconomics of Credit Money* (Cambridge: Cambridge University Press, 1988); C. J. Niggle, 'The Evolution of Money, Financial Institutions, and Monetary Economics', *Journal of Economic Issues*, Vol. 24, No. 2, June 1990, pp. 443–450.

42 Information on plan targets for bank lending is not available, but it is commonly acknowledged by Chinese policy-makers and researchers that they are seldom met. For instance, the actual level of bank lending is reported to have overshot the plan target by 23 per cent in 1989 and 89 per cent in 1990. See Ma and Sun (1991), pp. 221–223. For discussion of the poor performance of implementing bank credit targets, see also Tan Y. H. and Cao W. L., 'A Macro Analysis of Our Country's Problem of Circulating Capital', *Gaige* (*Reform*), No. 4, 1991, pp. 28–35; *Jinrong Yanjiu* (*Financial Research*), No. 19, 1991, p. 43.

43 Deaton argues that systematic studies on saving in developing countries are rare due to problems of conceptual measurement and pervasive data inadequacies. China is no exception. There is a general lack of understanding of saving behaviour both at the household and aggregate level in China. A. Deaton, 'Saving in Developing Countries: Theories and Review', *Proceedings of the World Bank Annual Conference on Development Economics 1989*, pp. 61–96. For a sectoral study of China's household savings in selected provinces, see G. Ma, 'Macroeconomic Disequilibrium, Structural Changes, Household Saving, and Money Demand in China', *Journal of Development Economics*, Vol. 41, No. 1, June 1993, pp. 115–136.

44 The reasons for the loss of control of bank lending at that time were many. One major policy-induced factor was the announcement by the central bank that, under the newly introduced system of controlling the gap between total bank lending and deposits, the 1985 annual lending level would be based on the 1984 year-end loan balance achieved by each specialised bank. Given the compartmentalised nature of the banking system and the economic and political pressure to expand loans to support investment, banks quickly turned that policy into a credit explosion.

45 O. K. Tam (1987), 'The Development of China's Financial System', *Australian Journal of Chinese Affairs*, No. 17, January; Y. C. Jao, 'The Financial System of China and Hong Kong', *Pacific Economic Papers*, 1990.

46 Working capital loans accounted for about 80 per cent of all lending by the specialised banks. See Ma Hong and Sun Shangqing (eds), *Economic Situation and Prospects of China 1989–1990* (in Chinese) (Beijing: Zhongguo Fazhan Chubanshe, 1990).

47 *Jinrong Yanjiu* (*Financial Research*), No. 11, 1993, pp. 7–8.

48 People's Bank of China, *Zhongguo Jinrong Zhanwang 1994* (*1994 Financial Prospects of China*), p. 19.
49 See, for example, T. Yuan *et al.*, 'An Analysis of Anti-inflation Fiscal Policies', *Gaige* (*Reform*), No. 3, 1989, pp. 78–84.
50 The most important of which are the rural industrial enterprises. For discussion of the growth of the rural industrial sector see, for example, W. A. Byrd and L. Qingsong (eds), *China's Rural Industry: Structures, Development and Reform* (Oxford University Press, 1990).
51 See O. K. Tam, 'A Private Bank In China', *The China Quarterly*, No. 131, September 1992.
52 Jefferson and Rawski argued that such behaviour can now be detected among state enterprises as their profitability converges to the non-state sectors. G. H. Jefferson and T. G. Rawski, *A Theory of Economic Reform* (Mimeo: University of Pittsburgh, 1992).
53 O. K. Tam, 'Capital Market Development in China', *World Development*, May (1991).
54 Tam (1992).

2

POLICY CHOICES OF THE CENTRAL BANK

Goals, Instruments and Effects of Central Bank Controls

Ou Jiawa

1 INTRODUCTION

The central bank in China, the People's Bank of China (PBC) was established in 1983. The PBC has since begun a long learning process in the making of monetary policies and in using various policy instruments. Since great emphasis was placed by the Chinese government on the 'special characteristics' of China's economy, the PBC has initiated many special experiments. It is not easy to make fair assessments of these experiments, because the environment for the conducting of these experiments is complex and difficult. The interpretation of these experiences and the degree of willingness to accept foreign ideas and knowledge among Chinese central bankers and economists are divergent. Many issues about the goals of monetary policies, policy instruments and reform designed for the future are based on these divergent understandings, and they remain controversial.

It is commonly recognised that the central bank has a responsibility for reaching a rational balance among three goals, which are: (1) security, including security and stability of financial institutions and of the macroeconomy; (2) efficiency of the financial system; and (3) promoting the healthy, efficient and stable development of the economy. None of them should be over-emphasised by sacrificing the others. But this recognition is not consistent with the traditional ideology that has been popular in China for dozens of years. Mao Zedong, the former Party Chairman, once declared that during any period, one and only one of the main contradictions should be grasped and solved and then all other contradictions would be solved smoothly and automatically. Banking practices in recent years seem to be the outcome of this mode of thinking.

The dependence of the PBC on political leaders and government accentuated such a bias. Under this mode of operation, planners can always pool enough resources to solve single economic problems at a time. They may therefore believe that they have a strong problem-solving capability, while detached observers may in fact have quite a contrary assessment. The biases of policy goals and instrument choices have always jeopardised other 'non-priority' contradictions, resulting in a cyclical shifting between contradictions that has led to worse situations.

With the experiences gained in recent years, the PBC may learn gradually that a central bank should make a more balanced choice of policy goals and appropriate policy instruments for serving balanced multi-objectives. A fundamental condition for making the right choices is an understanding of the functions of those instruments. How far and how fast improvement can be made will depend on the talents of PBC economists and their positions, as well as finding a rational balance between 'learning by doing' and 'learning through reading'. There is a dangerous tendency among some officials to deny the necessity of learning. They believe that China is too special to learn from experiences in other parts of the world.

The rest of this chapter is organised as follows: sections 2 and 3 will describe the policy goals and policy instruments of the PBC during two periods: from 1983, to the inflation peak in September 1988 and the anti-inflation period in 1990. Section 4 will try to analyse the mode of thinking affecting PBC choices of goals and instruments. Finally, section 5 will provide some thoughts on how it may become more rational.

2 EVOLUTION OF CENTRAL BANK POLICIES BEFORE SEPTEMBER 1988

China's central bank was established in September 1983. The main purpose was to separate PBC's control function of banking business from the operations of specialised commercial banks, in order to strengthen macroeconomic management and monetary policies. From the beginning, in formulating its responsibility for monetary policy, the PBC started using reserve ratio, interest rate management and rationing PBC credits to specialised banks as policy instruments.[1] However, the PBC inherited and employed more direct controls in the early stages of its development. They included making plans for directed loans, commanding specialised banks, as well as directly intervening in the management of their personnel and/or establishing branches of those banks. A learning process was needed for setting goals for PBC policies and related instruments. More important were the reform efforts to create a new financial environment suitable for the market-oriented changes of the national economy.[2]

Around the time of the Third Plenum of the 12th Chinese Communist Party Central Committee when the reform decision was made, a more fundamental banking reform was clearly needed and this was placed on the agenda. In November 1984, a leading group for financial reform was formed, headed by the Premier. The basic ideas for further reform were as follows:

1 Enterprisation of commercial banks, which means adopting the enterprise principles of autonomous management, separating from government operations and taking responsibility for their own profits and losses, etc.
2 Diversifying banking and non-banking financial institutions, which means going beyond the limitation of only four specialised banks and allowing new entrants into the financial system.
3 Paying more attention to indirect measures by the PBC for carrying out monetary policies.
4 Developing financial markets (primary and secondary) and related financial products, including a money market, a foreign exchange retention market and a capital market at a later stage. Financial markets with new independent entrants were understood to be needed for fostering fair competition and efficiency as well as providing a basis for indirect regulation by the PBC.[3] Government-directed loans can also be implemented by establishing some policy-purpose financial institutions connected to the financing of budgetary outlays rather than by commercial banks.[4]

Based on the new principles, the four specialised banks had become more commercial, some new entrants were allowed (see Table 2.1) and lending scope for each bank was expanded to promote competition. Many non-bank institutions such as trust and investment companies and securities companies emerged. These new entrants have lessened restrictions on business

Table 2.1 Bank and non-bank financial institutions

Institution	Before reform	After reform
Commercial/universal banks	4	12 (1992)
Trust investment companies	0	>700 (1992)
Joint-venture finance companies	0	2
Subsidiaries and representative offices of foreign banks	0	23
Housing saving banks	0	2
Securities companies	0	95
Rural credit unions*	60,000 (1985)	98,000 (1992)
Urban credit unions	0	4,000 (1992)
Trust and investment companies	0	386
Financial companies	0	17

Source: Almanac of China's Finance and Banking, 1989
Note: * Rural credit unions are under the leadership of the Agricultural Bank of China

scopes, brought more competition, more efficiency-minded bankers and less monopoly. Money market, including inter-bank lending and borrowing, short-term security and some kinds of deposit certificates, were introduced in many cities. The establishment of a capital market was the result of a common effort by the Security Exchange Executive Council (SEEC) and a few municipal governments. However, not all the new principles were put into action.

Preparation for breaking the high concentration of the four specialised banks in banking business failed to take place. Table 2.2 shows that by the end of 1988 the top four banks' combined shares of deposits and lending were still as high as 93 per cent and 94 per cent. It was difficult to realign existing sectional interests, as

Table 2.2 Concentration percentage ratio of China's four major banks (year end balance, 1988)

	Industrial and Commercial Bank of China	Agricultural Bank of China	Bank of China	People's Construction Bank of China	Total of the four banks
Deposits	43	21	24*	5*	93
Lending	43	23	25*	3*	94

Source: Almanac of China's Finance and Banking, 1989
Note: * Because of differences in the definitions of official data, these are estimates by the author

Table 2.3 Composition of securities
(billion yuan, balance at the end of 1989)

Type of security	Total cumulative amount issued	Outstanding balance
Treasury bonds	45.4	39.9
Other MOF bonds	13.2	13.2
Bonds of central ministries	21.5	21.5
Financial bonds authorised by PBC	16.0	8.5
Local corporate bonds	16.0	10.0

Source: Financial Management Department, People's Bank of China

many officials in the PBC came from the four major banks. The plan of establishing policy-purpose credit institutions for supplying special export credit, poor region credit, credit for some producers of public goods and priority industries, had failed, too. The specialised banks like to have both a commercial role and governmental functions, in fact believed by some to be an exclusive advantage of Chinese banks.[5] They insist on maintaining their capabilities in covering all kinds of credit.

The preliminary development of financial markets provided a basis for the PBC to start open-market operations in transmitting its interest rate policy. But the existing contradiction between the PBC and MOF (Ministry of Finance) led to a reluctance by the PBC to use treasury bonds as market instruments. Meanwhile, the PBC tried to develop financial bonds issued by PBC-supervised banks or institutions (see Table 2.3).

The financial reform mentioned above, and the enterprise reform, which raised operational financial autonomy, should have created a new environment where interest rates could work and become meaningful for both lenders and borrowers. The PBC introduced a series of adjustments in interest rates and realignments of rate structure for different terms and usages (see Table 2.4). However, progress in this respect had been slow and the rates were still below the equilibrium level. The PBC therefore continued to depend mainly on controlling interest rates by commands rather than by indirect guidance. That was one reason why the public and firms were not confident in the functioning of the rates and values of their monetary assets.

From 1983 to the summer of 1988 the most important instru-

Table 2.4 Interest rates (yearly percentage rate)

	1981	1987	1992
Firm's demand deposit	1.80	1.80	1.80
Firm's time deposit	5.04	6.48	7.56
Credit to firms	2.52	7.92	8.64
Household demand deposit	2.88	2.88	1.80
Household time deposit	6.12	8.28	4.98

Note: The rates of time deposit are the average of three-year fixed-term deposit rates

ment of money supply control that the PBC could use was additional lending to commercial banks. Credit ceilings and their rationing were sometimes used. Interest rates played an auxiliary role. After two years of experiments in 1979 and 1980, a new principle of 'unified plan and hierarchical management', under which lending volume was determined by the amount of deposits and target control on the difference between lending and deposits, was put into effect. This principle emphasised the autonomous decision making of local bank branches on lending, and adherence to the limit on the difference between lending and deposit levels, the difference being subject to quantity rationing through PBC's additional lendings.

From 1985, the PBC adopted a revised principle of a 'unified plan, dividing bank liabilities into blocks for each branch for their independent operations, establishing horizontal inter-bank lending relations and vertical regulation between the PBC and banks, as well as between bank headquarters and branches, and developing an inter-bank market'. In 1985, bank loan ceilings were used to curb the overheated expansions by decomposing M_0 and M_2[6] targets into targets for each bank and regional branch. Later on, ceiling control was relaxed. In the middle of 1986, ceiling control was shifted to the decomposed credit target used for fixed capital investment. In 1987, this ceiling applied to both M_0 and credits used in fixed capital investment.

Lending rates and rates of PBC *additional loans* (to specialised banks) have generally been lower than the levels needed for demand control and have even been negative in real terms, despite several upward adjustments. Interest rate changes have not been effective in money supply control or in allocating bank credits.

Under the distorted price system, commercial banks and their branches had a motivation to supply more credits to those manufacturing and processing sectors which profited from the distorted prices. This biased expansion caused the State Planning Commission (SPC) to put more budgetary funds and directed loans to its priority sectors (often less profitable or loss-making basic industries and infrastructure because of distorted prices) for reaching a better balance of industrial structure. PBC's loans to the banks and credit ceilings were decomposed into blocks and distributed mainly to provincial governments.

Under the specific incentive scheme and power structure at that time, local authorities had a strong motivation to invest in profitable sectors and to protect local industries and employment through protectionist measures which led to market segmentation. Local authorities were quite capable of intervening in the affairs of local branches of the PBC. Therefore, there were serious difficulties for the PBC in controlling money supply and in optimising credit structure, especially under the condition of tight money policy, when local governments tended to cut off bank credits that were not directly related to the generation of local revenues (often more important for central and/or national interest).[7] The inconsistency of incentives and conflicts in co-ordination became clearer in the observed administration behaviours after 1985. Such behaviours exhibited certain characteristics in timing such that programmes to control money supply were always aborted early and a policy cycle became inevitable.[8]

As to the exchange rate, balance of payments and the supervision of external debt, the PBC introduced a series of policy measures. Its authority and relations *vis-à-vis* the SPC, MOF and MOFERT (Ministry of Foreign Economic Relations and Trade) were gradually being clarified. However, the PBC was always a bit slow in policy-making. First, PBC's policy actions often lagged behind needs. Exchange rates have not been adjusted appropriately to levels close to the equilibrium rate, with the result that real exchange rate appreciation always occurred along with price inflation. The bank was slow to implement necessary actions to deal with external debt and balance of payments.[9] Second, some key PBC officials were slow in their understanding and recognition of these policy issues and they lagged behind reform changes. Some of them did not believe exchange rates can regulate Chinese imports and exports. They were negative towards rate adjustment. This had caused a great deal of difficulties to trade reform and trade policy formation.

Some PBC staff attributed the poor implementation of monetary policy to an over-dependence of the central bank on government. In China, the PBC has not been an independent institution. However, this chapter suggests that the concept of independence should be examined at two levels. At one level, independent procedure in a central bank means economic analyses and policy designing that are separated from governmental and/or political goals. This in turn means a key role for economists and experts in the central bank who are not interested in a political career. At the higher level, organisational independence of the central bank means reducing organisational pressure from the political side to a minimum. In China, we do not have this higher level of independence for the PBC. Before explaining that issue, we can examine what PBC could do by itself at the lower level.

Actual observations show that the PBC did not pay enough attention to educating its staff in seeking more professional careers rather than political promotions. Economists and experts were rarely seen in the PBC. Some older staff members said they were cadres of the government and the Party and were therefore no different from officials in other ministries. The top leaders of the PBC could have insulated its experts from political pressure, but this was not the case. On some occasions, when the PBC should be expected to propose restraints to counter the unwise thinking of the government's myopic decisions or misunderstanding of central bank functions in basic economics, it failed to perform appropriately and might even side with the government. It is fair to say that the PBC has now put more emphasis on educating a younger generation of experts and bankers. The position of economists in the PBC has also improved. But these minor improvements should not be considered as substantive changes. I believe that the role of economists in the PBC is very important for more scientific, independent analyses of economic situations and policy choices. This is especially true when a large part of PBC staff were inherited from its traditional mode of mono-banking, and who did not often operate from the perspective of macroeconomic considerations.

During the period of 1984–5, the Chinese economy gradually became overheated: money supply in terms of M_1 increased by an estimated 40 per cent in the second half of 1984. The overheating enthusiasm came mainly from local governments, while the central authority also made some mistakes. In February 1985, the State Council announced a decision to curb overheated investments during a Bank Governors' Meeting. However, real actions by the PBC could be seen only in July after four serious warnings and directives from four further Governors' Meetings. The problem in the PBC was that it failed to judge timely changes in microeconomic behaviour and macroeconomic troubles. It failed to prepare policy instruments for dealing with the new situations. Measures should have been taken to make local bankers respond to the PBC rather than obey local government wishes. Thus, the PBC was ineffectual in curbing overheated demand during this period and the government had to depend on political commands at the four Governors' Meetings. According to this author's observations from experience, the frequency of these kinds of high-level meeting was uniquely high.

After the imposition of administrative control over aggregate demand for six months in the spring of 1986, some factories fell idle because of a shortage of working capital credit. A typical example was the Hitachi colour TV factory in Fuzhou whose products were still in strong demand. The central government meanwhile started preparing a major reform package that included prices, taxation, public finance, trade and the banking system. Many Chinese economists believed that the programme should be accompanied by a tighter monetary policy stand. However, political leaders were not experienced in dealing with monetary problems arising from radical reform. They, together with the PBC, rushed to ease the problem of credit shortage, and dozens of billions of RMB credit beyond the original plan were expanded in spring 1986. The stabilisation goal as the top priority of monetary policy formulated in the summer of 1985 was actually terminated. As a result, the price index went up once again at the end of 1986.

In the summer of 1987, the State Council accepted a so-called twin-tightening policy of tight money and tight budget expenditure, but it lasted less than three months. From the end of 1986 to the spring of 1988, some top leaders in the government mistakenly believed that price movements in China were unique and special. Changes in the price index were thought to be unrelated to money supply, but only correlated to official price adjustments decided by the government. It was not unusual for top leaders to make such an anti-economics judgement, since they never had a systematic education in economics. Moreover, they tried to make decisions on subjective judgement, as available data samples on the reform transition period were far from adequate.

What was abnormal was that the central bank did not raise any strong objections and counter arguments, and did not at least stand together with many leading economists to say no to such misconceived judgements. The danger of that mistaken belief was quite clear. Expansion of money supply was adopted to gain a high growth rate while price reform was postponed in order to avoid inflation. The rationale behind the policy stand was that China had extremely special characteristics where economic theory or experiences in other parts of the world were irrelevant and rarely applicable. Published papers and documents at the end of 1987 and beginning of 1988, including the document of the Second Plenum of the 13th Central Committee of the Party, clearly showed this wishful thinking.[11] An inflation crisis was therefore inevitable.

3 INFLATION CRISIS AND ANTI-INFLATION MEASURES

The price index started going up significantly from the beginning of 1988, leading finally to a crisis of panic buying when inflation peaked in early September. It lasted around twenty days. An anti-inflation period followed. The necessity for effective control on aggregate demand became a consensus view among most economists and officials. However, there were still two different explanations as to how inflation came about.

The first argued that the decision on a radical price reform formulated during May–August 1987 was the source. The second attributed it mainly to the lax monetary policy. For a better understanding of how inflation came and went, this chapter will test several propositions against the statistical evidence. Note that the monthly (or quarterly) consumer price index used by the statistical authority in China is defined as the *weighted average* of the month divided by that of the corresponding month in the previous year.[12] This definition may be more suitable for an agricultural economy, as it fails to reveal fast changes – it under-reports when an inflation quickly comes and goes. Thus, we need a month by month (or quarter by quarter) index for more precise understanding and

Table 2.5 Quarterly percentage change in consumer prices

Year	1st Q	2nd Q	3rd Q	4th Q
1985	6.01	2.35	0.723	1.294
1986	1.89	-1.11	1.997	3.332
1987	1.224	1.042	2.094	4.481
1988	3.541	5.484	9.887	5.568
1989	3.212	1.475	0.754	0.830
1990	0.207	0.783	—	—

Source and method: See note[12]

analyses. This chapter provides a recalculated series for this purpose in Table 2.5. The recalculation was done by a simple transformation and an estimation on seasonal distribution of the base year 1984. Since the yearly inflation rates in 1983 and 1984 were reported to be only 2 per cent, the estimation would not bring a significant bias for recalculated data about 1988 and 1989.

Figure 2.1 presents the recalculated annualised quarterly price change rates from Table 2.5 and the official rates. The recalculated rates show a more defined pattern of rises and declines than the official rates. More importantly, the recalculated rates indicate much earlier and greater jumps during 1986, 1987 and 1988. A relationship between price change and credit expansions can also be detected from the recalculated rates. Three credit expansions occurred in the second half of 1984, early 1986 and late 1987, each followed by a significant price jump with a time lag of about six months. Austerity programs were introduced in 1985, summer 1987 and autumn 1989. There is no support for the argument by some officials that changing the money supply in China had no effect on inflation or anti-inflation because of the persistent shortages and public ownership in a socialist economy.[13]

However, in September 1988, Chinese top leaders had to reconsider the relationship between money supply expansion and inflation in the light of the clear feedback. A consensus was reached that effective control of aggregate demand was badly needed and that further reform would depend on a stabilisation program. Since then, a series of stabilisation measures has been introduced. Some measures are effective and widely accepted as correct, others are controversial in terms of their effectiveness and trade-off with negative impacts.

This chapter argues that anti-inflation policies, depending on the

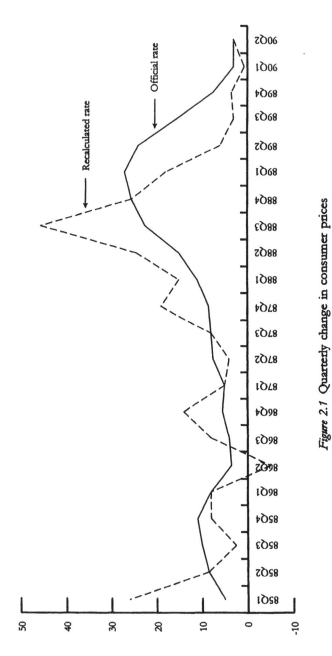

Figure 2.1 Quarterly change in consumer prices

Source: Recalculated price change rates are from Table 2.5 and annualised. Official price change rates are from SSB, *Monthly Bulletin of Statistics-China.*

choice of policy package, require different time spans to achieve the desired results (e.g. a currency reform for rapidly cutting off monetary overhang, or an austerity programme for absorbing the overhang gradually), and should not be subject to political will or command. Authority was probably over-zealous in its haste to curb inflation. A target was set to reduce the inflation rate to less than 10 per cent within a year. There was a tendency to apply too many curbs simultaneously, while some of them might produce serious negative effects. Quick short-term cures were chosen while long-term remedies were neglected. The PBC should have been responsible for analysing those choices and presenting rational proposals. Those measures and instruments in the anti-inflation package are discussed below. My comments will focus only on those related to the PBC.

A large number of investment projects were either postponed, suspended or cancelled. Total investment in real terms in 1989 was estimated to be 30 per cent lower than in 1988. Authorisation for project approval was recentralised to a large extent. Ceilings on the size of investment were issued to each province and large city.

The determination of quite a number of product prices was shifted from free markets back to fixed pricing, or to price adjustments subject to the approval of the price authorities. Local governments were instructed, as a political task, to take responsibility for controlling the local price index. It is questionable whether this local control was wise or not.

A considerable number of commercial enterprises in domestic trade, foreign trade and material handling were to be suspended, though the actual implementation has been much more difficult. These firms were believed to have committed price-raising behaviour that contributed greatly to inflation. It was also decided that a considerable number of investment and trust companies were to be suspended, cancelled or postponed, though there were a lot of difficulties in dealing with their assets and liabilities. These companies were believed to have created excessive funds in fuelling the overheated investment environment. It is questionable whether these investment companies could create money as commercial banks did.

Government-directed loans were substantially increased. Some of them were directed by the SPC, some by the PBC. Bank deposit rates were raised, and the three-year term rates were indexed to the inflation rate. Banks' lending rates were also raised, but remained basically negative in real terms in 1988 and early 1989. I believe that the interest rate policy works well and contributed a lot to anti-inflation efforts. A question lies in the calculation of the indexed interest rate.

In China, interest rates for three-year deposits have been an average rate rather than a compound rate. However, inflation rates over three years will produce an accumulative compound effect, thus the long-term deposit rates are still negative in real terms. In addition, as explained before, the statistical method of sampling and weighting in the calculation of the rate of inflation tends to produce under-estimates for the true rate. Another problem is that the interest rates are pegged to the official rate of inflation, which usually lags behind real price movements (as illustrated in Figure 2.1). The inherent time lag in the reported rate has an impact on deposit behaviour. The effectiveness of PBC monetary policy is similarly affected.

Credit ceilings, credit rationing and quantity control of the central bank lending to specialised banks became very important instruments for tightening money supply. Those measures, I believe, were necessary for the time being. Meanwhile, a careful study by the PBC is needed to determine the appropriateness of continuing dependence on them and when the emphasis should be shifted to some more efficient measures.

The enterprisation programme of the specialised banks and their branches has now been terminated. The specialised banks were asked not to behave as commercial banks. They should not only be responsible for their profits and losses, but also for implementing government policies under the direct instructions of the PBC, especially in the implementation of directed and priority lending according to the ranking issued by the SPC. Credit allocations were to be based not just on economic benefits, but also on social benefits. The four specialised banks are now called 'The National Specialised Banks'. This new, or shall I say traditional, principle may clearly be preferred by CPE officials and CPE economists. However, the principle creates confusion and incompatibility in terms of incentive and may provide opportunities for the exploitation of policy loopholes. It was difficult to understand why the PBC insisted on such changes and was so confident of their desirability. When these specialised banks operate as quasi-governmental institutions, it will be more difficult to manage money supply and to improve the security and efficiency of the banking system. It should also be rationally expected to present a more dangerous situation for the PBC. However, some officials at the PBC were confident that the PBC's direct leadership of those banks is more convenient and simpler than using other indirect instruments in commanding them to join in common efforts with the PBC to attain social benefits.

The inter-bank money market was drastically curtailed, as shown in Table 2.6. This market had been criticised for raising interest rates and was considered to be inflationary because lenders and borrowers were always profit-driven. Profits are seen to have come ultimately from higher interest rates in lending to the final borrowers (producers). The market was also thought to have created a loophole in controls over credit ceilings, and produced greater difficulty in financing directed loans. It became a source of financing for extra-plan projects and activities. All these issues should be carefully reviewed and considered by the PBC.

Because of credit ceilings and their rigid rationing, the control of product prices, and the strengthening of plan targets for producers, some enterprises started to encounter financial difficulties. Provincial-level governments began to intervene to slow down the settlement of inter-bank payments to other provinces for the purpose of retaining greater liquidity for their local banks. This behaviour caused more financial difficulties for the large state-owned enterprises, which provide products economy-wide, than for those supplying only the local market. Inter-firm debts emerged and developed. With the inflation of recent years, planned expenditures in the state budget for key investment projects became deficient, so that the managers of some of these projects (actually the SPC) delayed or refused to pay, or underpaid their purchases of equipments and/or materials produced by other

Table 2.6 The rise and fall of the inter-bank money market: estimated lending volume (billion yuan)

1985	0
1986	30
1987	230
1988	5,000
1989	300

Source: Financial Management Department, People's Bank of China

69

state-owned large enterprises. This developed mainly in early 1989. The affected industrial enterprises sought responses from both local government and local banks on whether they should reduce production and ask for settlement of over due payments owed to them by other enterprises (as they did in 1986), or just simply keep on producing (which means expanding borrowing through working capital loans from banks) and allow financial insolvency to exist and develop.

It was not surprising to see that local governments wanted their enterprises to keep on running to avoid unemployment, especially in the sensitive time after June 1989. It was also reasonable for them to argue that many debts were caused by other provinces and some central authorities. It may not be apparent why commercial banks and their branches could allow these debts and keep expanding new credits to cover old debts. However, the behaviour becomes more understandable if we take into account the new changes in bank functions which have become policy-oriented and aligned with the Chinese government's social objectives and priorities of directed loans.

In addition, there were four factors facilitating such behaviour. First, local governments' influences on bank credit are still strong. Second, the incentive scheme for bank branches was closely connected to their interest revenues. Even if borrowers pay interest in advance, the repayment of principals may still be in great danger of becoming bad debt. The problem is that local branches do not have a strong incentive-compatible responsibility or criteria to ensure credit quality. They can always go up to the head offices in Beijing, which are more policy-oriented. Third, after a large amount of investment credit had been cut off and with the relatively higher rates of deposit absorbing increased savings, the head offices of the specialised banks and the PBC had surplus funds for supporting these loan expansions. Fourth, while the central government asked local governments to make political and economic stability the top priority, this pressure was not applied on banking business, although indirect impacts were also significant.

It seems to me that when the PBC emphasised the priority of monetary stability and security at macroeconomic level, it left out microeconomic security. There existed no effective policy to deal with the insolvency problem. As a result, mountains of inter-firm debts grew quickly, and though some clearing efforts had been made by local governments and local branches of the PBC, the situation continued to worsen.[14] Actually, some banks or branches would have probably fallen into insolvency if it was not for the credit expansion which temporarily hid the troubles.

The real exchange rate had been depreciating continually prior to December 1989. According to official statistics on the rate of inflation, the real RMB exchange rate had depreciated around 55 per cent in the domestic market in the period between the two rate adjustments in July 1986 and December 1989. Export subsidies, though they still existed, were reduced substantially to 4 per cent of total export value (according to the memorandum of China to GATT in 1987) and this amount had been fixed since the beginning of 1987 under the contractual responsibility system. Thus, exporters faced greater financial difficulties with the worsening inflation and the over-valuation in the nominal RMB exchange rate. The trade authority had been asking strongly and repeatedly for adjustments in the nominal exchange rate in order to keep the real exchange rate stable. However, officials in the PBC had not been positive towards the rate adjustment. They had three reasons. First, RMB depreciation was inflationary. Second, they believed that the rate was not important and that Chinese imports and exports had very low price elasticities. Third, the performance of import–export and trade firms is the responsibility of MOFERT (Ministry of Foreign Economic Relations and Trade), not the PBC.

The rate adjustment of 21 per cent in December 1989 could be said to be too late and of too little magnitude. Before this depreciation, some exporting firms were caught between fulfilling planned targets for exports and financial self-sufficiency. A few firms started to give preference to meeting plan targets and to observing financial discipline under the contractual responsibility system. Thus, they kept on exporting by rolling over their bank borrowings and allowing their insolvency to persist and develop. They might have speculated that the official exchange rate had to be changed. However, the change came too late and was smaller than they expected, and was far from enough to cover their insolvent debt. Meanwhile, credits for exporting were made a top priority in the national credit policy, so that these insolvent trade firms could remain afloat or even become more 'price-competitive'. The timid adjustment in the exchange rate could not stop this behaviour of the export firms, and other trading firms followed the pattern. For the banks, a more serious problem with the trading firms (compared with industrial producers) was that many have a relatively small amount of capital in comparison with their turnover. Thus, their insolvency problem would rarely be resolved and their borrowings were highly likely to turn into bad debt. However, some PBC officials have argued that the insolvency problem is the responsibility of MOF, MOFERT and local governments and that the PBC cannot help.

In short, an unsatisfactory balance between macroeconomic and microeconomic security, banking efficiency and promotion of economic development seems to have emerged in recent years in terms of PBC policies and policy instruments. Some kind of policy cycle will probably continue. This chapter suggests that the slow pace of economic reform might be the reason for many difficulties we are facing, including imbalances in economic growth and instability.

By the end of 1989, the official rate of quarterly inflation was brought down to 0.83 per cent according to the recalculation in Table 2.5 (its annualised rate would be 3.36 per cent). This outcome was better than many people had expected. However, output growth had dropped sharply and its monthly growth rate had become negative since October. Thus, many related problems arose. These trends continued in the beginning of 1990. A package of new growth-promoting policies was decided in March 1990. We can analyse the reasons for the recent development of PBC policies and its underlying orientation.

While the PBC is responsible for carrying out anti-cyclic measures against periodical oscillation, it seems to have responded to changes a bit slower than was needed. The bias in the official statistics on the price level may be one of the reasons. The PBC started to increase credits sharply in December 1989, and again after March 1990. It should be noted that a slow response is likely to produce an inappropriate amplitude for anti-cyclic purposes. If an anti-cyclic measure is slow in phasing in, it might be worse than doing nothing.

In March 1990, a package of seven policy measures was announced for creating easier money and speeding up growth. It included providing more bank credits; lowering interest rates; increasing credit for state purchasing by commercial, foreign trade and raw material handling firms; clearing inter-firm debts; and increasing investments. While some economists thought that the money supply was too tight and aggregate demand too low at the end of 1989, others tried to show that the credit expansion since December 1989 might be too strong and too rushed.[15] I believe that the essential reason for the recession was not well analysed and understood. The recovery policy at the end of 1989, which depended on a large credit expansion, would not be as effective as predicted because the expansion was too rapid and too strong. The growth in M_1 was much higher than GDP growth, and since autumn 1989 the gap between M_1 and GDP growth rates has been among the biggest.

One controversial policy was the so-called 'reservoir role' assigned to the firms in domestic trade, foreign trade and material handling (firms in raw materials and capital goods with a role to support plan targets in key projects and key production). 'Reservoir' means absorbing production surplus by raising inventory which will be released in periods of excess demand. One serious question is how to identify if the increased inventory will meet future demand or not. Another question is when a commercial firm becomes a government agency for implementing this kind of intervention, who should pay for the cost of increased inventory? The principle for firms to become financially self-sufficient presents another question. The operations of these trade firms greatly depend on bank credits, since their capital/debt ratios are very low. The building of their inventory has therefore to be supported financially by bank credits. Indeed, most risks associated with 'reservoir' activities are ultimately borne by the central bank. How the PBC and the 'national specialised banks' treat these increasing demands of credit becomes a crucial problem.

When the traditional planning authority undertakes anti-cyclic actions, they are not really concerned with the security of the banking system and the insolvency problem of trading firms. However, it is now a very substantial problem for bankers to evaluate the repayment capability of those firms which were given credits to build up supporting inventory. One of the central bank's responsibilities is to monitor the credit positions of commercial banks. However, it is clear that the tradition of asking firms and commercial banks to behave as government agencies is still predominant and as such they are more compatible with the requirements of a centrally planned economy (CPE). Once again, the PBC does not seem to have achieved a balanced position as far as monetary goals and financial disciplines are concerned.

One of the reform goals has been to change socialist enterprises with soft budget constraints (as defined by J. Kornai) to entities with hard budget constraints.[16] It is incorrect to say that all capitalist firms lie at the extreme of the hard constraint status, while all socialist firms lie at the extreme of the soft constraint status. Many Chinese firms are now in between the two extremes after years of reform. This chapter therefore suggests that the transition should be measured by a continuous variable rather than by a binary status. However, some recent observations have revealed that the extent and the scope of the soft budget constraint phenomenon have significantly enlarged with the financial support of bank credit. In China, many economists have criticised socialist enterprises for lacking self-discipline, but this chapter stresses that such enterprises should be constrained by a variety of external forces, mainly via ownership, laws, regulations and policies, as well as the banking system. When governments at different levels became increasingly paternalistic and banks continued to expand credit to accommodate repayment problems of borrowers, the enterprises would certainly not be interested in self-discipline. This recent trend is becoming a big problem. Even for the short term, this development is costly and poses a serious obstacle to further reform, since many enterprises have learned a lot about how to seek help from government and banks.

4 THE MODE OF THINKING IN POLICY CHOICES

This section analyses the reasons why the policy choices discussed in previous sections were made in order to provide an understanding of the underlying mode of economic thinking. Such an understanding will be helpful for predictions of future development.

A very common belief during China's socialist economic reform is the virtue of combining the advantages of plan and market. This concept seems quite simple and reasonable, especially for those who believe there are many potential advantages in a CPE. The most important issue is how to identify the advantages and disadvantages in the two economic systems. A better combination must be formulated on the basis of correct understandings, and a well considered design incorporating a feasible co-ordination of the selected elements from the two systems. In reality, however, the theoretical and empirical analyses in this respect in China have been far from adequate.

The traditional mode of thinking was based on observations of the early stages of development of the market economy. The CPE's way of thinking still dominated the minds of many Chinese economists and policy-makers. Such ideas are not well supported by empirical observations of economic evolutions. Falsely identified advantages and disadvantages created many problematic combinations, which led to sub-optimal and unsatisfactory outcomes. The concepts of policy co-ordination, feasibility and incentive compatibility are still very weak among China's policy-makers. The real practice is mainly a process of trial and error.

Traditionally, government responsibilities were divided among ministries which were organised along economic sectors. Banking was managed by a banking headquarters, and later on, by the PBC. The management of prices and their changes, as well as the inflation rate, were the duties of the price authority. Imports and exports and their financial flows were managed by the foreign trade ministry. Domestic trade was managed by the ministry of commerce. Industrial enterprises were managed by different industrial ministries according to economic sectors. The economic reform did not change this division, though some improvements in cross-sector cross-function co-ordination have been made.

It is interesting to note, therefore, that the PBC seems to be more concerned with banking operations, but less with inflation, balance of trade, aggregate level of production, inventory and sales. Indeed, some of China's top leaders are also more accustomed to check with the price authority when inflation occurs, or with MOFERT when export volume slumps. An interesting example of institutional reform in government organisation happened in 1988. A proposal was suggested to merge the price authority with the PBC for better results in regulating monetary conditions. The response was that it was a strange idea to put two unrelated economic management areas together. The PBC expressed the view that it did not have any intention to 'eat rice from the same bowl' with another department. That can explain why the PBC does not worry too much about the impacts of its monetary policies on areas that are formally the responsibility of other ministries, and why sometimes the PBC was slow in adjusting its credit and exchange rate policies.

Industrial policies, which assign different priorities and policy treatments for different sectors, can be found in the development process of Japan and Korea, and are very attractive to and easily accepted by planners in China. A kind of bias has emerged where the successful experiences in Japan and Korea have been praised loudly, even louder than in Japan and Korea. The cost and distortions associated with industrial policy are rarely heard about in China. In recent years, industrial policies have become very popular and are accepted as a key factor in reaching an organic combination of planned economy with market regulations. Industrial policies provide the basis for existing distortions to continue. This can explain why the PBC and the 'national specialised banks' are active in carrying out government directed loans. Even the PBC likes to manage its own credit priority policies. However, observations and analysis in a study show another picture[17]. It is found that industrial policies are far from adequate in compensating for the existing price distortions. Any product that suffers an artificially low price set by a control authority has a 95 per cent probability of belonging to the preferred sector under the industrial policies, and vice versa.[18] This chapter suggests that the central planners, including those planners for directed loans in the PBC, have limited resources of talent and time. If they try to substitute the roles of market and prices, they can hardly channel their limited resources to the most important task of policy-making.

The central planners used to assume that most officials in the hierarchical bureaucratic structure are good and competent cadres, and that the central plan can therefore be decomposed into hierarchical targets which can be fulfilled under local/sectoral supervision and regulation. When people lost confidence in the traditional CPE and started economic reform to seek a better combination of plan and market, that old assumption was still widely and unconsciously held. There has always been a strong tendency to assign government agencies to solve many economic problems, including 'chaoses' created by economic reform. Thus, the programme of industrial policies, directed loans, the 'national' roles of large banks and so on are much emphasised. However, the practice of 'seeking personal benefits through administrative power' is extensive and widely reported in China.

When a wide range of central controls are strengthened, we have to ask these questions: whether officials in charge can get enough information for decision-making in an increasingly diversified economy; whether they use the opportunity to seek more economic rents for personal gain, or to serve the public interest. However, the traditional mode of thinking does not put the administration task and administrative behaviour together. It does not consider motivation, incentive, competence and loopholes for official-led implementation. A simpler concept adopted is that all officials are and should be communists serving the people. In the banking sector, the PBC may like to be a direct 'commander' of all banks rather than a regulator.

As a commander, the PBC has a stronger position than a regulator. First, it can issue orders instead of using indirect policy instruments. Second, it can directly assign and/or remove executives and leaders in specialised banks. Third, for many important decisions, banks have to report and seek approval from the 'commander', although they have nominal decision-making power under China's banking regulations. When the four specialised banks were established the PBC believed that they would serve social goals and would not just be seeking profit. The possibility that they do not behave in this way was not raised.

In the field of policy analysis and policy assessment, the 'cost-plus' price formula is widely accepted and used in China. This mode of thinking is based on the traditional socialist price theory where pricing depends on the sum of input costs and an average profit rate. The optimisation of resource allocation is a completely separate affair in the planning process, without any connection to prices. The cost-plus formula also supports the argument that if there are no changes in input costs, then no inflation can happen, with no consideration given to aggregate balance of demand and supply.

When officials discuss a reform policy, they can therefore always reach a negative assessment by referring to analyses which inevitably stress only the consequent rise in cost and small benefit. For example, in discussing the need to raise interest rates and exchange rates in an inflationary period, such increases are believed to create higher costs for borrowing and imports of inputs, which will in turn induce price rises in many final products. Thus, the cost or risk of this adjustment policy is seen very clearly to be inflationary only. They are not quite sure about what benefits can be gained. For instance, there are benefits from the reduced budget subsidies for exports, though importers may ask for more. The reform economists suggest that less distortions in those rates can improve allocative efficiency of scarce resources, thus bringing a significant benefit. But this concept is not widely understood and accepted as suitable for China in the traditional thinking mode.

Therefore, reform proposals for reducing distortions have always been made from a weak political position. It may explain why the adjustment of interest rates and exchange rates is slower than needed.

It is argued by some that the price elasticities for both supply and demand are very low in China, which are regarded as the special characteristics of China's economy. This assertion goes further to repudiate the benefits that can be gained from reforms to reduce distortions, including those in interest rates and exchange rates.[19] Reforms to reduce distortions always involve reform of microeconomic behaviour, while reducing distortions is the precondition for reformulating microeconomic behaviour. Thus, it is really difficult to know the exact elasticities beforehand, because the actual values are always greater than the *ex-ante* estimation based on the data of past behaviour. However, there are misleading analyses and subjective assertions about the very low elasticities which are quite wrong, and they are done without carefully tested evidence. Such opinions have impeded reform decisions on interest rates and exchange rates many times.[20]

Finally, the traditional Chinese economics textbooks described market competition as a source of speculation and anarchical chaos, and as contributing to unequal income distributions. This way of thinking still has a great influence. Whenever price speculations, 'chaoses' and unfair income distributions happened in the inflation period, and whenever banks and investment companies made money in the overheated investment climate, many analysts would attribute the source of all sins to market competition. Thus it is argued that competition and the entry of many new financial institutions, especially investment companies, must be reduced. In businesses such as insurance and specific fields of investment, state monopoly is still available and regarded by some to be better than competition because of the perceived superior order and control. When some economists suggest that we strengthen competition to gain more equal income distributions, lower prices and to reduce the current rent-seeking activities, traditional officials ridicule such ideas.

5 FUTURE DEVELOPMENT

While there are many different opinions on the future development of China's financial system and on the way for further reform, and though there are some obstacles to that mode of thinking, the process of economic development and the direction of reform in China are subject to Deng Xiaoping's principle that 'practice is the only criteria for checking any theory'. Any misconceived opinions or policies have to be corrected based on the feedback from practices or a practice-proven theory. Meanwhile, the policy of reform and opening to the outside world will provide further chances for testing and to conduct comparative studies on international experiences. Therefore, this chapter predicts that all things will converge gradually on a correct understanding and a logical evolution. As for the financial sector, we will probably see progress in the following areas.

China's economic reforms have been summarised by many economists as a market-oriented reform. Though since the anti-inflation period the Chinese government has adopted the new slogan of 'combining the planned economy with market regulation', it does not change the direction of reform, which has been moving toward a greater role for the market mechanism than ever before. Therefore, the market-oriented reform is not changed and this orientation will become clearer for those who had no understanding about where the reform will go. This orientation and reform development will also be applicable in reforming the financial system.

The principle of being responsible for one's own profits and losses will be more effective with a programme to harden budget constraints. Bank loans will be decided mainly on the profit-making capability of borrowers. The inter-firm debt and/or pure debts problems must be solved resolutely. Debt–equity swaps might be considered as a method.

The commercial banks will continue their reform through a process of enterprisation. New entries and competition will be prudently allowed. The insolvency problems in some banks and financial institutions must be solved.

The PBC will be more experienced in balancing divergent policy goals, which consist mainly of security (both macroeconomic stability and microeconomic safety of the banking system), efficiency and promotion of economic development. It will no longer focus on only one contradiction in one period. The PBC will realise that indirect control instruments are more effective and have more secure outcomes. Along with the reform process, more indirect instruments will be used by the PBC.

In creating a new environment for banking business, the PBC will pay more balanced attention to keeping stability, making regulations and supervising. Both the paternalism and excessive intervention from the PBC will be reduced. Economists and other financial experts will play a more important role and gain their positions in the PBC for more independent and scientific thinking on issues of monetary policy, policy instruments and co-ordination with other macroeconomic policies.

The RMB will become a convertible currency. It might start in the trade account, and later on in other accounts. The PBC will realise the importance of this step.

Notes

Most data in this chapter came from the *Statistical Yearbook of China* and the *Almanac of China's Finance and Banking* of recent years.

1 Ren Junyin (1989) 'The Basis of China's Banking System', C. Kessides *et. al.* (eds), *Financial Reform in Socialist Economies* (Washington, DC: The World Bank, 1989).

2 Liu Hongru (1988) *Zhongguo Jinrong Gaige (China's Financial Reform)* (Beijing: Chinese Financial Press).

3 Wu Jinglian, Zhou Xiaochuan (1988), *The Integrated Design of China's Economic Reform* (Beijing: Zhanhuan Chubanshe).

4 Xu Meizheng (1987) 'Structural Reform and Financial Reform in China', in C. Kessides *et. al.* (eds), *Financial Reform in Socialist Economies*, 1989.

5 Zhou Xiaochuan (1986) 'Import-Export Bank and Policy-oriented Finance', in Zhou Xiaochuan, *Research on Foreign Trade Reform* (Beijing: Zhanhuan Chubanshe, 1990).

6 M_0 = cash currency (balance); M_1 approximately = M_0 + demand deposits (balance).

7 The central government may command local governors to reduce the total amount of bank loans in their regions through their administrative interventions. Local officials then consider what kind of loans they may seek to suspend through their influence and actually tend to reduce those related more to central interests.

8 Qiao Qing (1989) 'Carefully Review the Experiences and Continue Deepening Financial Reform', in Hong Yuncheng and Xu Shuxin (eds), *Carry Out the Policy of Retrenchment and Reform for Doing Better Financial Jobs* (Beijing: Chinese Financial Press, 1990).

9 Zhou Xiaochuan, Zhu Li (1986) 'China's Banking System: Current Status, Perspective on Reform', *Journal of Comparative Economics*, No. 11, 1987, pp. 399–409.

10 Wu Jinglian, Hu Ji (1988) *The Dynamic Analysis and Policy Study for China's Economy* (Beijing: People's University Publisher).

11 See the published documents and newspapers about the Second

Plenum of the 13th Chinese Communist Party Central Committee, February 1988.

12 We can define the following:

$P_{t,m}$ = price level of tth year and m^{th} month
$PX_{t,m}$ = monthly price index
P_t = yearly average price index
S_i = sale revenue of ith good
P_i = price of ith good

$$P = \sum_{i=1}^{380} S_i * P_i, \text{ then } PX_{t,m} = P_{t,m}/P_{t-1,m}$$

$$PX_t = 1/12 \sum_{m=1}^{12} P_{t,m}$$

(Basket contains around 380 important goods.)

We are not satisfied with using $PX_{t,m}$ (the official figures). We would like to see another index such as $PXX_{t,m}$, such that $PXX_{t,m}$ = $P_{t,m}/P_{t,m-1}$.

Now we have all data of $PX_{t,m}$ (t = 1985, 1989; m = 1,12) and $PX_{1990,m}$ (m = 1, 5) from statistical reports, if we have $P_{1984,m}$ (m = 1, 12), we can calculate all $P_{t,m}$. The statistical authority has not published $P_{1984,m}$, probably because of a lack of experience in data collection of the base year, and because the method and the basket have been changed since 1985. Now we can get a small basket sample of monthly prices in 1984 from some regional reports (internal). Using such data, we can estimate $P_{1984,m}$. From that estimation of the base year, a transformation to calculate all $P_{t,m}$ can be carried out, then all $PXX_{t,m}$ can be obtained. In Table 2.5, quarterly figures are given.

13 Li Yining (1988) *The Clue for Economic Reform* (Beijing: Zhanhuan Chubanshe).

14 Zhou Zhengqing (1990) 'On the Formulation and Policies of the Inter-firm Debts', *People's Daily*, June 8, 1989, p. 6. (Zhou Zhengqing was the vice president of the PBC.)

15 For the former view, see Yang Peixin, 'Leading Experts Discuss Problems in National Economy', *Hong Kong Wen Wei Po*, 28 April 1990, p. 3. For the latter view, see Wu Jinglian, 'Stepping Up Economic Readjustment Through In-depth Reform', *Economic Report* (Hong Kong), No. 3, 1990, pp. 11–12, and Liu Guoguang, 'Some Considerations on the Relationship Between Economic Ratification and Deepening Reform', *Renmin Ribao (People's Daily)*, 2 February 1990, p. 6. The latter two suggested the possibility of another round of inflation by that credit expansion.

16 The notion of soft budget constraint is from Kornai (1980); see J. Kornai, *The Economics of Shortage* (Chinese edition) Beijing: (Economic Science Press, 1985).

17 Zhou Xiaochuan, 'On the Computation and Applications of Computed Accounting Prices', *Financial Economics*, No. 6, 1987.

18 The price authority had a list showing goods with regulated low

prices, and the SPC had a list of encouraged production and investment in industrial policy (published in *People's Daily*). An unpublished comparison was made by the SPC showing a high correlation between the two lists.

19 A challenging question for some econometricians is whether or not the forty-year time series data can be used to estimate these price elasticities. The old CPE mechanism decided a zero elasticity in the former thirty years, and a very low elasticity on average in the forty-year observations. The recent time series data may not provide a sufficient sample for these estimations, and these small sample data do not look persuasive.

20 Zhou Xiaochuan (1985) 'Model of National Economy and the Decomposing Approach of Large-scale Economic System', in *Doctoral Dissertations* (Beijing: Qinghua University Press, 1987).

3

CHINA'S ECONOMIC AND FINANCIAL REFORM

Wu Jinglian

In China's economic reforms since 1979, financial reform has been prominent. After ten years, the financial mode of the traditional command economy has undergone great changes. New financial organisations have been established. New financial means and new financial measures have developed and have, to a certain extent, been able to meet the financial needs of those state enterprises which have obtained some autonomy rights, and the non-state enterprises which have rapidly developed over recent years. However, the new financial system is obviously only in its preliminary stages and has still not been able to operate efficiently as a complete system. Moreover, a new mechanism for macroeconomic adjustment has not been established to replace the old system. This has led to macroeconomic chaos since 1985, and calls for renewed recentralisation have grown louder. This chapter discusses the basic experiences of ten years of financial reform, and in particular analyses the relationship between financial reform and the economic reform in general.

1 BASIC FACTS ON THE REFORM OF THE FINANCIAL SYSTEM

In the process of the ten years of reform, China's financial system has undergone the following changes.

1.1 Major changes to the source of investment finance

Since 1956, with China's transition towards a socialist economy, the financing of China's enterprises came principally from the state budget. Additional investment in fixed assets and working capital

Table 3.1 Major source* of funds for fixed capital investment in state
enterprises (percentage), 1970–90

	State budget	Self-raised funds	Domestic credit
1970	75.3	23.9	0.8
1975	64.4	34.0	1.6
1979	61.4	31.1	3.6
1980	44.7	36.5	11.7
1981	38.6	42.4	13.6
1982	31.4	45.3	16.2
1983	35.9	43.5	14.3
1984	35.3	43.4	15.4
1985	26.4	40.4	23.0
1986	22.2	38.4	22.7
1987	20.6	38.2	24.6
1988	14.7	40.5	24.2
1989	13.4	42.8	20.9
1990	13.2	42.1	23.6

Source: SSB: *Statistical Yearbook of China,* various issues

Note: * Foreign and other sources of funds are not included

funds (working capital quotas) of the enterprises were all made
through budgetary grants. Only the temporary capital funds (non-
quota working capital) came through short-term credit from the
People's Bank of China. The principal part of budgetary investment came from the central government budget. Immediately after
the 1958 and 1970 devolution (*xiafang*), the budgetary shares to
regional governments were increased somewhat. Since the beginning of the economic reform, investment funds originating from
the budget have gradually decreased. To accommodate this decline
the portion of finance provided by the banks has significantly
increased. As Table 3.1 indicates, prior to 1979, more than 60
per cent of investment in fixed assets of state enterprises came
from budgetary grants. By 1985 this had decreased to one quarter,
and after that it decreased further.

The main source of bank funds came from the increase in
household saving deposits. From 1978 to 1988, household saving
deposits increased by an average rate of 30.5 per cent per annum.
In the previous twenty-five years, the average annual rate of growth
was less than 11 per cent. As a proportion of the aggregate source
of funds in the state banking system, household saving deposits
increased from 9.37 per cent in 1979 to 30.84 per cent in 1990 (see
Table 3.2).

Table 3.2 Source of funds in state banks (percentage), 1979–90

	1979	1985	1989	1990
1 Deposits, of which:	61.96	66.45	66.19	69.16
Enterprise deposit	27.75	32.21	22.65	23.74
Budgetary deposit	6.88	5.73	3.22	2.26
Household savings*	9.37	16.45	27.42	30.84
Government	8.55	5.06	3.55	3.65
departments and units				
Rural deposit	9.42	6.99	5.26	5.05
Others	–	–	4.08	3.62
2 Bonds	–	–	0.51	0.55
3 Liabilities to international	–	1.22	1.02	1.10
financial organisations				
4 Currency	12.38	15.36	17.21	15.70
5 Own funds	19.79	12.10	8.79	7.81
6 Others	5.87	4.88	6.27	5.67
Total	100	100	100	100

Source: SSB: *Statistical Yearbook of China*, various issues

Note: * This represents mainly urban household saving deposits as most rural households place their savings with the rural credit co-operative (RCC) systems. The share of rural household saving deposit, in the total source of funds of the RCC was 36.3% in 1979, 77.9% in 1985 and 84.6% in 1989.

1.2 Changes to the structure of financial institutions

Prior to 1979, China practised the Soviet-style mono-banking system. The People's Bank of China, apart from being responsible for monetary control as a central bank, handled almost all lending business, including industrial, commercial and rural credits. Some specialised banks did exist. However, they were actually either agents for budgetary grants handed down by the Ministry of Finance or business branches of the People's Bank of China. For example, the People's Construction Bank of China, founded in 1954, was in fact the cashier of the Capital Construction Finance Department of the Ministry of Finance, and the Bank of China, established in 1949, was in fact the international business department of the People's Bank of China. All deposits of state enterprises had to be held in accounts at the People's Bank. Credit could only be obtained there. All business transactions between enterprises had to be settled through the People's Bank according to the state plan. The payment of wages could only be made through a separate 'wage fund' account, the quota of which was stipulated by the state plan and the withdrawal of cash from that account was under the supervision of the bank.

From 1979, the People's Bank began to separate out its non-central banking business. The independence of the Bank of China was strengthened. In early 1979 the People's Construction Bank of China was re-established and began running a pilot scheme of interest-bearing investment loans. At the same time the Agricultural Bank of China was restored to handle the business of rural deposits and credits. In 1984, as urban reform began in accordance with a decision by the State Council, the People's Bank of China set up the Industrial and Commercial Bank of China to handle urban saving deposits and loans for working capital and medium-term credit for equipment to enterprises. The People's Bank of China has been thus freed to function as the central bank, concentrating its efforts in analysing and making macro-monetary policy, strengthening its control over the financial markets and maintaining monetary stability.

Apart from the national specialised banks, many diversified forms of banks and non-banking financial institutions were established. From the end of the 1970s, rural credit co-operatives were widely restored and developed. In 1980 the People's Insurance Company of China re-established domestic insurance, which had been discontinued for twenty years. After 1984, regional banks, trust and investment companies, leasing companies and other non-bank financial institutions were set up. In 1987 two national banks, the Communications Bank based in Shanghai and the CITIC Bank, a subsidiary of CITIC, were established. Thus, the pattern of a two-tier banking system with the central bank separated from ordinary banks gradually emerged.

1.3 Changes to the highly centralised and bureaucratically controlled bank funds management system

Prior to the economic reform, bank funds were administered through a system of so-called 'unified deposit and unified lending'. That is to say, all deposits had to be, tier after tier, handed up to the head office of the People's Bank of China, while credit was granted and broken down at each tier according to plan. In April 1979 the State Council approved and circulated the 'Memorandum of the National Meeting of the Local Branch Heads of the People's Bank of China.' According to this document, bank credit funds were to be managed under a new method of control 'under unified plans, administered at different levels, the establishment of a link between deposits and loans, and control over differences between bank loans and bank deposits'. Thus, the Head Office of the People's Bank would, according to the state-approved credit plan, assign the target amount of the annual difference (gap) between credit and deposits at its provincial-level branches. Then, according to the stipulated figures, it could establish control over 'the differences between bank loans and bank deposits'.

In February 1981, 'control over the differences between bank loans and bank deposits' was changed to 'the contract responsibility system for an agreed amount on the difference between bank lending and bank deposits'. That is, the various branches could, within the scope of the contracted difference between bank loans and deposits ratified by the head bank, extend credit on the basis of the level of deposit so that 'the higher the level of deposit the larger the amount of credit could be extended'. In 1985 this developed into the method of 'unified planning, control of bank lending by separate categories, establishing that lending could only be permitted when there was an equivalent actual amount of deposit, and the establishment of inter-bank lending'. The central bank designated credit funds (that is, bank's own capital base) to the specialised banks. The head offices of the various specialised banks similarly allocated these credit funds to their local branches within their organisations. When funds of the specialised banks were insufficient, they could then borrow from other specialised banks and could also apply to the central bank for additional loans. In this way, dealing in funds between banks, between the upper and lower levels of the banks, and between the commercial banks and the central bank became one of borrowing and lending.

At the same time, the financial reform changed the former administrative methods under which it was principally the state which made grants of fixed asset funds and working capital funds to state enterprises. From 1985, on the basis of several years of experimentation, funding for basic construction investment was changed from state budget grants to bank loans. The change from grants to credit (*bo gai dai*) was implemented by the People's Construction Bank of China according to the state plan for capital construction. There were regulated interest rates and loans were to be repaid over years. At the same time, according to a decision by the State Council in June 1983, all state enterprises' working capital requirements would be gradually met by bank credits.

1.4 Diversification of financial assets and development of financial markets

The increase in household saving deposits and the broadening of financial activities of the enterprises demanded new financial instruments. In 1980 Shanghai was the first to begin a pilot scheme of commercial bill discounting. In 1985 this was popularised on a national basis. In 1986 the People's Bank of China developed re-discounting activities and permitted the market trading of commercial bills. From 1981, the issue of public bonds (treasury bonds) was re-introduced, and after that business in re-discounting and trading of public bonds was developed.

In 1987 twenty-nine cities opened up short-term markets for enterprise bonds. Thus, various kinds of bank bonds and enterprise bonds began to appear in the financial markets. Together with the emergence of the markets for public and private securities, some securities companies were established.

Thus, to all appearances, a new financial system had begun to take shape. However, if we were to investigate the actual operation, we would find very quickly that in comparison with the financial systems of most market economies, this was more of form, rather than of substance. In China, an integrated financial market, incorporating short-term and long-term financial markets, has not been formed. Credit activities are mainly under the control of centralised planning, originating from the top and handed down tier by tier to the localities. At the same time, financial institutions have not been able to develop as independent managers of money capital. The central bank has difficulty in acting as the co-ordinator and the mediator of the financial market, but performs like a bureaucratic organisation of the government system, taking on many administrative functions.

2 REASONS FOR THE SLOW PROGRESS IN FINANCIAL REFORM

The slow formation of financial markets and a financial system appropriate to a market economy is a universal phenomena in those countries of Eastern Europe which have been carrying out economic reform. The common explanation is that because of ideological reasons or theoretical confusion, the reformers of these countries only recognised the necessity of establishing a commodity market (goods and services), but neglected the need for the development of financial markets, and in particular, the establishment of a long-term financial market (a market for capital). Consequently, they were said to have neither put reform of the financial system onto the agenda nor adopted necessary measures. As I see it, this explanation is incomplete. At least it is insufficient to explain the main reason for the tardiness of China's financial reform.

Actually, as early as 1984, some Chinese economists advocated hastening financial reform by establishing financial markets and a modern financial system as a 'breakthrough' to further the reform process. Moreover, they raised the basic issues and considerations for the proposal of a blueprint for this reform. Further discussions of these issues and proposal were made in the first half of 1985.[1]

As everyone knows, prior to 1984, the main idea that guided China's economic reform was to 'devolve authority to and share profits with' the regional governments, departments and enterprises. Expansion of their autonomy was the basic content of the whole reform. In 1984, reform to the enterprises through 'devolving authority and sharing profits' reached a peak. What was unexpected was that just as everybody was preparing jubilantly to welcome a comprehensive all-out advance in reform, serious inflation suddenly emerged. Beginning from early 1985, China's economy entered a period of retrenchment, and various reforms that were originally planned for implementation basically stopped for 'readjustment'. Chinese reformers, in summarising the lessons, gave many explanations why the reforms met with setbacks. The earliest hypothesis to explain the economic chaos was that 'the extent of deregulation in the microeconomic sphere has exceeded the increase in the capacity of macroeconomic control'. So in order to raise the capability of macroeconomic control, some economists advocated the establishment of a modern financial system suited to 'a planned commodity economy' (viz. a market economy with macro-management should be the thrust of further financial reform). According to modern Western market models, such a financial system should include the following:

1 A financial market where competition exists. The short-term and long-term finance of enterprises would basically be satisfied

through interaction in such a market. There should be no barrier to entry, and the price of money (interest rates) would be decided through competition.

2 Within the scope regulated by financial law, competitive commercial banks and non-banking financial institutions would operate autonomously and in accordance with the situation in the short-term money market and the long-term capital market. Whether they lend or not, or how much they lend, would be decided upon independently. At the same time they would be responsible for their own profit and loss, and for the economic consequences of their management.

3 The function of the central bank is principally to guarantee monetary stability by carrying out its function independently. The central bank is not to intervene in the specific business operations of the commercial banks, but through adjustment to the re-discount rates, the regulation of bank reserve ratio, open market operations and other conventional market economy measures, to adjust and influence the activities of the commercial banks.

These ideas received support from many economists. At the time, enthusiastic discussions were focused on the establishment of a long-term capital market, particularly the stock exchange. It was envisaged that once the capital market was established, not only could optimal re-allocation of resources be quickly realised, the central bank could, moreover, through open market operations, greatly strengthen its macroeconomic control. Specific plans and measures were discussed, including topics such as the appropriate scale of commercial banks, and the establishment and management of the stock exchange. But in their exposition of ideas to make financial reform 'a breakthrough point', Chinese economists and officials of the financial and monetary administration found that reform to the financial system was severely constrained by other aspects of reform. At that time, genuine markets for goods and services had not been formed. Under a seriously distorted price system, there was no way of realising such a programme of financial reform. The main reasons can be summarised as follows:

1 The exchange of commodities (goods and services) is conducted mainly on the spot at a point in time, while in the money market the exchange of monetary purchasing power takes place at different points in time. Therefore, when the prices in commod-

ity markets are not set through competition and are seriously distorted, there cannot be rationalisation for the price of money (interest rates).

2 In a situation where commodity prices and short-term interest rates are irrational, it is impossible to rely upon the market mechanism to adjust the actions of lenders and the activities of the banks so that their own interests are in conformity with the demands of society. In such a situation, the enterprisation of the management of the banks can only be illusory.

3 The effective operation of the capital market is even more difficult. As the relative prices of various commodities do not reflect their relative scarcity, high profitability of enterprises very often does not result from improvements to management but is derived from some type of 'rent-seeking' rights. In such a situation one does not know where to begin to obtain the correct valuation of capital (capitalised expected returns). It is even more impossible to guide the flow of capital through its price, into the most efficient areas, and to realise the optimal distribution and re-allocation of resources.

In the discussions of Chinese reform economists during the first half of 1985, a viewpoint that gained dominance was that the reform process should go through a certain sequence, and that at every stage in the sequence all aspects of the reform would necessarily be co-ordinated and synchronised.[2] This viewpoint was reflected in the 'Proposal for the Seventh Five-year Plan' (1986–90) at the National Congress of the Communist Party of China in September 1985. The proposal demanded that during the period of the Seventh Five-year Plan, reform to the economic system be carried out unswervingly, cautiously and safely so as to establish within the period a basis for a new economic system (i.e. a 'planned commodity economy'). The proposal considered that in order to achieve this the following three co-ordinated sets of reforms had to be grasped. First, state-owned enterprises should become autonomous entities responsible for their own profits and losses. Second, efforts should be made to further develop the commodity market, and to gradually improve the market mechanism in factor markets, including the financial market and the labour market. Third, the management of the economy by the state should change from direct control of the enterprises' activities to indirect control, through the use of economic levers such as fiscal and credit policies as well as legal rules to control and adjust the operations of the national economy.

According to the above decisions, in the summer of 1986 the Economic Reform Office of the Chinese government ('The Office of Research for Economic System Reform of the State Council') drafted a co-ordinated reform plan encompassing prices, the taxation system, the fiscal system, the financial system and the domestic and international trade system, which it planned to put into operation from early 1987. The characteristic of this proposal was to co-ordinate price reform, tax reform and fiscal reform as the basis of the entire reform:

1 *Price reform*: first of all, on the basis that in 1986 it was necessary to continue to tighten the money supply, regardless of whether allowing for some adjustments first or complete deregulation at one point in time, the prices of the means of production of non-natural monopoly sectors (including raw materials, energy, transport and freights) were to be liberalised. Along with this, the prices of intermediate and finished products would also be liberalised. In this way, by the end of the Seventh Five-year Plan, with a few exceptions (such as grain, where the supply and demand price elasticity is very low and which will possibly continue to have a dual price for a long time to come) the prices of the majority of commodities could be liberalised.

2 *Tax reform*: abolish the 'one rate per enterprise', 'adjustment tax' and all subsidies. The principle of fair tax responsibility will be established. Value added tax (VAT) will replace the present, circulation tax with its disparate rates on different products and complex regulations. Apart from VAT, luxuries and restricted consumer goods such as wine and cigarettes will attract a special high tax rate. The government should impose a land tax for the use of state-owned land, and resource taxes for the use of state-owned natural resources (such as mineral resources, water resources, etc.).

3 *Reform to the fiscal system*: abolish the system whereby governments at all levels can, according to the scope of their administrative jurisdiction, demand revenue (taxes and profits) from the enterprises that they control. Change this to a distribution of revenue between the central government and the regional governments according to different types of tax. That is to say, under the premise of separation of the functions of the various

tiers of government and the functions of government enterprises, define those taxes which can affect the sectoral structure of the national economy (such as special consumption tax) as the special revenue of the central government. At the same time, define those revenues that are closely linked with the functions of level governments (such as land rent) to become the exclusive revenue of the local governments. Only neutral taxes (such as VAT) can constitute a common source of revenue, to be divided according to a unified proportion between the central and local governments. At the same time, set up a system of subsidies whereby fixed amounts of subsidies allocated by the central budget to the local budget are calculated according to a formula and special subsidies are given according to special needs.[3]

The above three reforms could to a great extent remove price distortion, and could also greatly weaken the incentive for local governments and departments to adopt protectionism. They could also provide a fair competitive environment for the enterprises. They could create a market basis for the government to employ policy priorities and administrative guides to realise industrial policy. These measures to strengthen competition are the same as those already proclaimed a few years before but, because of the lack of necessary market conditions, they could not be realised then.

Even more closely related to the questions discussed in this chapter is the establishment of basic market relations in order to create the preconditions for the development of the financial market and reform of the financial system. Consequently, financial reform was at the time considered an important component part for a market-oriented and co-ordinated reform programme, and a draft plan to push forward this reform was formulated.

In the autumn of 1986, after some revision, the above draft plan was approved by the Chinese government. Unfortunately, at the end of 1986, the leaders of the Chinese government changed their original reform strategy from that of co-ordinated reforms to a method of carrying out partial reform, with reform in enterprises as the central theme. They abandoned the concept of establishing the basis of a new system during the Seventh Five-year Plan, and suspended the co-ordinated reforms that were originally decided upon on 1 January 1987 with regard to prices, tax, public finance, finance and trade. This meant that financial reform could neither retreat nor continue. After this, some efforts of a partial nature were made, for example the establishment of a stock exchange in Shanghai and in certain regions pilot projects for the establishment of private banks were carried out. They were, however, insufficient to change the general structure. Because of the internal logic of the economic development already described, it is difficult for such efforts to produce effective results.

3 THE DISTORTIONS IN THE PRESENT FINANCIAL SYSTEM

For a long period of time, the economic reform strategies were based on 'devolving authority and sharing profits', advancing with single reform measures and schemes in the hope of a breakthrough to bring about new changes. As a result, the command economy and the market system have for a long time been locked in stalemate, with neither playing an effective role. The effect on the financial system does not only show itself in the tardiness of reform, but with distortions in it. From an overall point of view the main defects of the economic reforms reveal themselves in the present financial system.

First, the 'administrative nature of the division of power' has created a situation of multiple lines of authority over many affairs and market segmentation, which leads to fragmentation of the financial market and low investment efficiency. In China, for over a decade of economic reform, the characteristic of the command economy under which political control and management of enterprises are mixed has been essentially maintained. Nor has there been any fundamental change to the pattern where the administrative organisation decides everything. None the less, the decision-making powers of the central government have been decentralised to the various tiers of regional governments.

In 1979 there began a process of reform to 'devolve authority and share profits'. It 'decentralised' the majority of central enterprises and handed them over to the regional governments. Moreover, the former arrangement of the financial system, whereby the central fiscal authority 'took in all the profits and paid out accounts', was changed. According to its position in the vertical structure, an enterprise paid revenue to its tier of government (profits and taxes), and then the various tiers of government would pay the higher fiscal organisations a ratio or a certain quota of revenue.

The extensive 'decentralisation' of enterprises and fiscal resources at the beginning of the 1980s produced direct effects on the behaviour of the various tiers of government. From the provincial and city governments down to the village and county governments, all competed to set up factories and shops, duplicating distribution, with no consideration given to their inherent comparative advantages and the optimal economic scale for their projects. From the beginning of the 1980s, quite a number of provinces, cities, counties and even towns jumped in and set up cigarette factories and small breweries. In all, the 'new five small industries' fought for raw materials and energy with the larger industries. Later the craze for 'small aluminium factories', 'small charcoal factories', 'small oil refineries', 'small woollen mills', 'small cotton mills', continued to spread throughout the country, causing the regional economic structure of the national economy and the scale of enterprises to take a turn for the worse.

At the same time they fought bigger 'battles' for raw materials and export commodities. Because the export incentive mechanism is set up according to regions, some export enterprises were willing to raise the domestic purchase prices, then dump products abroad at lower prices, thus letting the 'bounty' flow in great quantities abroad. Then in order to protect these very inefficient industrial and commercial enterprises from going bankrupt and to obtain 'profits', the governments at various tiers used their administrative powers to carry out a protectionist policy for their own enterprises. They monopolised extremely scarce raw materials and energy, put up obstacles to prevent competing products from entering their own markets, and reduced and waived taxes for their own enterprises, giving them low interest loans and other preferential treatment. They supported them in carrying out unfair competition, creating serious market segmentation, so that those enterprises under the protective umbrella of administrative power became even more inefficient.

This system of 'division of administration' caused regional governments to interfere in the professional activities of the banks at various levels. They did their utmost to use bank loans to support their efforts in realizing the economic goals of the region. At the same time, for the following reasons, the banks at various levels had to co-operate actively with the regional governments:

1 The various branches of the specialised banks are all under the leadership of the various tiers of government (the various Party Committees) and the future prospects of the leading cadres of these banks are to a great extent decided upon by the regional governments and the Party Committees.

2 The lending capacity of the specialised banks at different levels in making loans depends upon the amount of re-lending given to them by the central bank, and this re-lending quota is none the less decided upon through negotiations with the centre and by the banks at the regional level together with the regional governments.

3 In China, under the system whereby enterprises repay loans before tax, how much of the loans local enterprises will repay annually is in fact arranged by the local financial authorities; that is to say, how much of the loans the banks can retrieve depends upon the decision of the local government.

4 At present, in a situation where the main allocative mechanism is through administrative means and not through the market, and in a situation where government interventions in all aspects of social activities have not changed, the establishment of a banking branch network, the employment and living quarters for bank employees, the education of the employees' children and their employment, all depend upon the local government.

Thus, out of the reformed Chinese financial system there has emerged the so-called 'regionalisation' tendency of the banks' business activities. Every bank branch has the tendency to make loans only to the enterprises under the same local regional government, and prevents money from flowing out, thus completely restricting the mobility of funds. In 1986, a survey by the Industrial and Commercial Bank of China of ten cities which had carried out pilot financial reforms[4] revealed:

1 With regard to the local banks, as the local government makes the decisions, 'loans of a compulsory nature', 'assigned loans', are many and varied. These include the 'base figure' loan of working capital for industrial and commercial enterprises, and investment loans of fixed capital assets for key local enterprises. Of these, the proportion of the general quota for loans for technical reform mandated by local government was as high as 50.29 per cent in 1985 and 73.34 per cent in 1986. Of this category of loans, there are a great number of borrowers who

are clearly known to have little ability to repay, but the banks still have no choice but to make the loans.

2 In the short-term inter-bank money market, the trend of regionalising capital usage was even more obvious. Of the transactions in the inter-bank market for the specialised banks surveyed, only 32 per cent were to financial institutions outside their own system. Financial institutions and trust investment companies outside the specialised bank system made 87 per cent of their loans to local enterprises.

Under such conditions the banks have become a powerful financial tool in support of this regional expansion drive. At the same time, the central bank (the People's Bank of China) cannot possibly control money supply through a unified financial market. Instead, it divided the monetary target among the local administrative areas and made local banks responsible for controlling money supply. In a situation where the aim of the monetary policy of the central bank is implemented through the dispersed control by the various regions, it is inevitable that they will compete to put money into circulation, creating the serious consequences of loss of control over the general volume of money and inflation.

There are in addition the serious price distortions created by the adoption of gradual adjustment and partial relaxation in price reform. This has caused chaos in the financial market and a return to administrative control measures time and again.

Due to the opposition of some people who upheld the 'planned price' system, efforts to carry out price reform in 1981 were frustrated. In early 1984 it was decided to use the method of 'dual track prices' with both 'planned prices' and 'negotiated prices' (which in the past existed outside the planned pricing on a very small scale) to gradually advance to a transition towards a market price system. As a result, the 'dual track' pricing system with almost every commodity having both a planned price and a market price has come into being. One commodity may have many prices with great disparity between the high and low prices. Later, because this 'dual track system' was seen by some people as 'having Chinese characteristics on the reform road', it became a fixed formula. Price reform was then abolished from the medium-term reform agenda. Since the middle of the 1980s, approximately half the total value of social commodities is sold at prices stipulated according to plan. More than 60 per cent of the means of production and less than 50 per cent of consumer goods are sold at planned prices.[5]

As a result of such a pricing system, the scarcer the commodity, the higher the degree of planned management and the higher the proportion sold at the planned price, the lower the average level of the price. On the other hand, the more abundant a commodity, and because the portion that is liberalised is comparatively larger, the relative price level is comparatively high. For instance, in 1990, as the proportion of planned control for crude oil was high, and as its planned price remained fixed at the same level as it was decades before, the general average price of every ton of crude oil at the official price calculated on the exchange rate was only equal to 20 per cent of the international price, while the price of petrochemical products was much higher than the prices of the international market. This cannot but create a serious distortion to the system of relative prices.

This serious distortion of prices has stimulated large quantities of investment to flow towards high-profit processing industries. In basic industries and infrastructure where profits are small or where there is even loss, they are short of investment and stagnate in growth. Over recent years, on the one hand, there has been one wave after another in investment into colour televisions, refrigerators, beer, aluminium cans, ethylene and other high-priced commodities. The newly created productive capacity has far outstripped rational demand, wasting large amounts of resources. On the other hand, the supply gap in agricultural products, raw materials, energy, communications and so on, which reap little profit or no profit, is growing larger. Many production facilities have to stop for lack of raw materials, electricity and transport, thus hindering the development of the entire national economy.

In a situation where the price system is seriously distorted, the adjustment in bank interest rates cannot at all guarantee the efficient allocation of resources. Consequently, there is no alternative but to adopt administrative co-ordination of the financial system: low interest rates on planned loans (substantially negative real rate), liberalise a part for free loans and utilise market interest rates. Some people believe that, as long as planned finance corresponds with the investment of planned products, and market finance corresponds with investment in free marketing, then there will be no distortion in the financial system. Actually it is very difficult for this system to work normally because it is impossible to separate clearly the above two areas and to link up the corresponding investments. The result is that there is rent seeking through exploiting the differential in commodity prices and in interest rates. According to calculations by one Chinese economist, in 1988 the value represented by the differential between official interest rates of Chinese state bank loans and market interest rates was as high as 113.88 billion yuan, which was 8.1 per cent of the GNP value of that year.[6]

Such kinds of rent-seeking activities in the exploitation of differentials in interest rates and rent-seeking activities in other areas have together over the past few years constituted the colossal economic basis for the increasing spread of corruption. As the figures in Table 3.3 suggest, together, the above forces have led to the loss of control over money supply and to the increasing pressure of inflation. From 1984 to 1988, China's economy experienced increasingly serious inflation, and in the autumn of 1988 there erupted throughout China panic buying and withdrawals of saving deposits.

When it was not possible to exercise effective management over the operation of the credit system through the market, China's monetary authorities have, in macroeconomic administration, tended mainly to retain the methods of administrative control. As a result, in managing credit and finance there has emerged control by both administrative and economic methods. On the one hand, the central bank continues to transmit to the head offices of the various specialised banks control targets for loan balances according to the plan of the national economy. The head offices of the specialised banks – according to the directions stipulated by the central bank – then transmit to their branches broken-down targets for loan balances. These are transmitted down to the sub-departments, the regions and sometimes even the branches within enterprises. On the other hand, the central

Table 3.3 Increase in money supply and the inflation rate (percentage)

	1983	1984	1985	1986	1987	1988	1989	1990
GNP growth rate	10.4	14.7	12.8	8.1	10.9	11.0	4.0	5.2
Increase in cash	20.7	49.4	24.7	23.3	19.4	46.7	9.8	12.8
Increase in Retail Prices Index	1.5	2.8	8.8	6.0	7.3	18.5	17.8	2.1

Source: SSB: *Statistical Yearbook of China,* various issues.

bank – through its own 'lending' facility and by changing the rates of the deposit reserve ratios of the specialised banks – will adjust the ability of the specialised banks to give credit. Specific items of loans are decided upon by the local banks. The bases for the operation of these two methods are different, and very often it is very difficult for them to be compatible, thus adding to the chaos.

In dealing with the serious inflation of 1988, the ideas which prevailed in 1989 and 1990 were those that advocated the further strengthening of administrative control. For instance, some advocated restoring and strengthening the administrative functions of the various specialised banks. Measures included those ratifying and releasing wage funds; restoring and strengthening the method of fixing the total quota of directed loans at each level and even issuing credit to designated enterprises; expanding the power of the ministries in examining and approving fixed assets investment, and so on. However, as a result of ten years of economic development and economic reform, the changes that have taken place in the degree of complexity of China's economy and the degree of its diversity are tremendous. It is extremely difficult to place one's hopes in forced administrative methods of control to improve the situation in the financial sector, especially if the aim is to fully mobilise funds, to have effective resource allocation and thus maintain long-term financial stability. Consequently more and more people are gradually coming to realise that the way to push forward financial reform is on the basis of a co-ordinated set of reforms to the economic system.

4 THE DIRECTION FOR DEEPENING THE REFORM

In accordance with the lessons learned from the past, financial reform of the future perhaps needs to grasp the following points:

1 The basis for the reform of the financial system is to see that the different reforms guarantee the formation of a commodity market and its effective operation. This includes reform to the enterprises and price systems. Consequently, in order to push forward financial reform, first of all there must be an effective breakthrough in the formation of a competitive commodity market. Reforms to the enterprises and price reform should

be carried out in sequence, one after the other, but should be carried out in co-ordination at the same time. For instance, as the first step, state enterprises should be made autonomous and responsible for their own profit and loss. The prices of all commodities, apart from an extremely small minority, should be liberalised. Under such conditions, the commodity market would then be able to begin preliminary operations. On this basis, the reform to the financial system could also take a comparatively large step forward. At the same time, pilot schemes to transform state enterprises into joint stock companies should be carried out. Preparatory work on various legislation should also be stepped up when the market system is operating in the expected stable stage, the large and medium state enterprises should gradually be changed into share holding enterprises.

2 The emphasis in deepening the reform of financial institutions is to consolidate the two-tier banking system of the central bank and commercial banks. Apart from continuing to develop banks and non-bank financial institutions outside the system of the specialised banks, the present local branches of the specialised banks should be reformed into competitive enterprises with profit and loss responsibility, autonomy in handling business, and in mutual competition. These banks should accept deposits, issue bonds as the main source of credit funding and not rely upon the central bank for everything. Whether loans are made or not and how much should be loaned and how high or low the interest rate should be, the bank should, according to the situation of the borrower and the market, decide autonomously.

3 Efforts should be made to further the growth of the financial market. First of all, through the enterprisation of the local banks and development of the non-bank financial institutions, and the more direct competition of business between the banks, monopoly should be broken down and market competition developed. At the same time, pilot schemes for stock exchanges should be run, and the scale for securities trading gradually expanded. Funds needed for profit-making enterprises would generally rely upon the financial market. As to the development of infrastructure and basic industries which require large sums of investment and have a long period of return, the government should establish a 'policy finance' funding organisation, which

may issue credit with low interest or no interest, with government subsidies.

4 Strengthen the central bank's adjustment mechanism. First of all, the branches of the People's Bank of China set up according to administrative regions should be changed and set up in central cities according to economic regions. Their connections with the local governments should be broken. The present system whereby the central bank provides funds to the specialised banks mainly through re-lending should be changed to one where there is bill discounting. The central bank should control money supply through a unified financial market.

Naturally, this does not exclude the retention for a definite period of some administrative guidance to the business of commercial banks, for instance, using something similar to the central bank of Japan's method of 'window guidance' to control the total level of credit of the commercial banks. When the central bank carries out its 'administrative guidance' it should only stipulate the total amount of investment of some sectors, or the total amount of credit for some industries. It should not exceed its functions and meddle in others' affairs and decide the specific projects to be given credit.

Notes

1 See Zhao Xiaomin, 'On the Establishment and Perfection of the Central Bank System'; Jiang Jiwu, 'A Re-examination of China's Socialist Banking System'; Lin Junyen, 'How China's Socialist Central Bank Can Play its Role Fully'; in Yi Hongren *et al.*, (eds), *Jinrong Gaige Lunwenji* (*Collected Papers on Financial Reform*) (Beijing: Chinese Financial Press, 1986).

2 Wu Jinglian, 'Progress by Single Measure or Coordinated Reform?' (Address to Conference on Central Committee of the Chinese Communist Party Draft Suggestions for the Seventh Five-year Plan, 15 July 1985.) See also Wu Jinglian, *Exploring the Issues of Economic Reform* (Beijing: Zhongguo Zhanwang Chubanshe, 1987), pp. 268–269; Guo Shuqing, Lou Jiwei and Lin Jirui, 'Study of the Overall Plan of Systematic Reform (August 1985)', in Wu Jinglian and Zhou Xiaochuan (eds), *A Complete Design for China's Economic Reform* (Beijing: Zhongguo Zhanwang Chubanshe, 1988), pp. 25–47.

3 See Lou Jiwei, Xiao Jie and Liu Liqun, 'Thoughts on Model of Economic Operation and Reform of Fiscal and Taxation System', in Wu and Zhou (eds) (1988); Lou Jiwei and Liu Liqun, 'Outline of Ways to Resolve the Budget Deficit Problem and Reform the Fiscal System', in Wu and Zhou (eds) (1988), pp. 111–151.

4 Zhang Xiaojie and Zhao Yujiang, *Finance: The Current Operational Mechanism and Its Reform* (Chengdu: Sichuan Renmin Chubanshe, 1988), pp. 236–247.

5 According to estimates by the State Statistical Bureau, within the total ex-factory output value of production materials in recent years, 60 per cent were at state-determined prices, and 40 per cent were at state-guided or market prices. Of the total retail sales, the proportion at state prices accounted for 31.3 per cent, guided prices 23.2 per cent and market prices 45.5 per cent. For the value of rural products, state prices accounted for 35.3 per cent, guided prices 24.3 per cent, market prices 40.4 per cent of the total. Guided price means that the government fixes the median, and the maximum or minimum price. State Bureau of Prices, *Chinese Yearbook of Price*, 1990.

6 Hu Heli, 'An Estimate of the Magnitude of Rent in 1988', *Jingji Shehui Tizhi Bijiao (Comparative Economic and Social Systems)*, No. 5, 1989, pp. 10–15.

4

ANALYSIS OF CHINA'S INTER-BANK MONEY MARKET

Xia Bin

1 BACKGROUND AND REVIEW

The essential feature of China's traditional credit management system was that it was centred around the state's credit and cash plans, whereby the bank branch network throughout the country draws up the plans for deposit taking, lending and cash receipts and outflows. These draft plans were submitted through the network from the local branches up to the financial authorities in charge, which after scrutiny and confirmation gave approval. All activities of the local branches including deposit taking, lending and cash management, were strictly subject to the approved plans. Deposit taking which surpassed the plan did not confer the right necessarily to extend more loans than stipulated by the plan, while surpassing the lending quota did not have to be related to the taking of deposits.

The state credit and cash plans were constantly adjusted during the course of the year to accommodate changes in the economy. This system had served to stifle the initiative of banks to bring in greater deposits and ruled out the possibility as well as the necessity of inter-bank activities. Since 1979, the bank credit management system has undergone various reforms so as to fit in with the development of the socialist commodity economy.

On 8 October 1984 the People's Bank of China (central bank) issued 'Rules for the Management of Credit Funds'. Its aim was to turn specialised banks into genuine economic entities responsible for their profit and loss, and to further strengthen and improve the macroeconomic management of the central bank, thus tackling the long-existing problem with the 'supply system of finance' (*gongji zhi*). The aim of the rules was to change the relationship between the central bank and the specialised banks from one based on direct supply of funds to repayable credit. The amount of lending will be linked to the level of total deposits. Overdrafts with the central bank will be disallowed. The Rules also encouraged inter-bank lending activities among all banks and across regions. It was only after the rules were effected that inter-bank activities on a nationwide basis gradually developed.

In January 1986, the State Commission for Economic Restructuring and the People's Bank of China jointly organised a workshop to review activities of the inter-bank market which had developed since 1985. Taking part were representatives from cities designated for banking reform experiments. It was confirmed that the development of the inter-bank market was a major component of financial reform. It was also made clear that the methods, maturities and interest rates of inter-bank lending would be negotiated and decided upon by the participants according to market conditions. The holding of this workshop accelerated the development of the inter-bank market across the country. In August 1986, the Shanghai branch of the Industrial and Commercial Bank of China formally announced the opening of the 'Shanghai Money Market'. On 4 October 1986, the People's Bank of China issued a notice specifying that all banking institutions have the right to lend and to borrow funds and that neither higher banking authorities nor local government should intervene in any way; and that inter-bank activities should be gradually promoted on a national scale. Subsequently, inter-bank activities of various kinds were initiated across the country. Inter-regional inter-bank lending networks were developed by branches of the same bank, money markets were organised jointly by financial institutions in the same city and inter-bank centres were created jointly by financial institutions in the same region.

Consider the city of Wuhan as an example. The first tier of inter-bank lending is represented by the money market organised by agreement among urban credit co-operatives of the city, the participants being the urban credit co-operatives operating there. The second tier is the money market organised by the Wuhan branch of the People's Bank of China, which also provides its floor-space. The clientele comes mainly from the various specialised banks of the city. The third tier consists of those specialised banks of Wuhan which participate in inter-regional financial networks on a national scale, such as the financial network established among twenty-seven cities along the Yangtze River or the national financial network of eleven major urban centres. By the end of 1987, some 360 'money markets', 'inter-bank lending centres' and 'financial networks' were to be found throughout the country.

The mode of professional activity of the 'markets', 'centres' and 'networks' across the country fall basically into two categories. The first comprises the visible markets. Most of these are engaged in inter-bank lending within the same city. During the stipulated trading time[1] the 'markets' provide trading space. On the exchange announcement board the names of borrowing and lending financial institutions are posted along with the intended amount, maturity and interest rates for the market participants. In these markets, participants find their own business partners, negotiate terms and reach agreement on transactions independently. The second category of professional activity comprises the invisible markets. Most of these handle non-local and inter-regional inter-bank lending and borrowing. During the stipulated trading time, financial institutions send information through tele-communications to the centre of the networks, receive feedback from the centre and then negotiate and execute transactions with other financial institutions.

These 360 'markets', 'centres' and 'networks' are independent of each other, and lack definite forms of liaison. The markets operate at different times, have differences in their mode of operations. Thus, when market imbalances appear on a particular business day in a particular market, the market often cannot be cleared through channels other than that particular market and must wait for the next designated business day. This has resulted in lost opportunities for inter-bank activities and the blocking of financial channels. To solve this problem proposals were made to set up five to six national money market intermediaries – finance companies acting as economic entities to handle inter-bank borrowing, bill discounting and trading of commercial papers. By the end of 1988, thirty-seven financial companies had been established and within one year they had handled funds of 30 billion yuan. The establishment of financial companies is in principle an inevitable outcome in the development of China's money markets. However, due to problems associated with accreditation, approval and management of the financial companies, plus the fear for the loss of control over the macroeconomy in 1988 as well as other factors, licences for all these thirty-seven companies were revoked by 1989. This move forced inter-bank activities back into the pre-1987 pattern where the 360 'markets', 'centres' and networks' acted as intermediaries. Since their inception, China's inter-bank markets have developed comparatively quickly, despite a number of setbacks. In 1986 the cumulative amount of inter-bank borrowing by the Industrial and Commercial Bank of China and the Agricultural Bank of China was 35 billion yuan, which was 20 per cent of the total incremental bank lending of that year. In 1987, cumulative inter-bank borrowing by all financial institutions throughout the country reached 200 billion yuan, which was equivalent to more than 39 per cent of the incremental bank lending of 144.2 billion yuan for the year. In 1988, inter-bank borrowing reached 524.1 billion yuan, which was 345 per cent of incremental bank lending of 151.9 billion yuan for the year.[2]

Regardless of the forms taken, the market orientation of the development is on the right track. The emergence of the inter-bank market has been a revolution as far as the country's financial system is concerned. It has broken the old credit management system where planned allocations from the central bank were handed down and where any inter-bank activity was completely ruled out, leading to low efficiency in funds allocation. The emerging inter-bank market has already shown advantages in adjusting financial balances across regions and among banks, in accommodating needs omitted from the state credit plan, in optimising funds allocation and in facilitating the more efficient use of funds.

2 ANALYSIS OF THE CHARACTERISTICS AND PROBLEMS OF THE INTER-BANK MARKET

China's inter-bank market came into existence in the special circumstances of the process of reforms to the price system, the enterprise system, the investment system and other economic systems. Therefore, certain unique phenomena different from other countries have unavoidably appeared, and are manifested in the problems and immaturity of this developing market.

(1) There is a lack of organic link between the 'markets', 'centres' and 'networks'. Most of them have no knowledge of the address, business time or scale of operation of other markets. This is due in part to the backwardness of telecommunications and the inadequacy of organisation by financial authorities. It is also due to the practice of protectionism both by local governments and by banks. If one locality set up a 'market', another would set up a 'centre',

terrified that if the locality or bank concerned did not establish an 'inter-bank centre' of its own, then capital would flow out to other places and other banks. Some localities have gone so far as to formulate rules for lending, giving preference to local financial institutions over non-local ones and intra-bank over inter-bank institutions. Segmentation and duplication of inter-bank markets throughout the country (for instance, there are thirteen city-level inter-bank markets operating in the city of Nanjing) are bound to cause two major problems. First, transactions are often duplicated in different markets before reaching their final destination, leading to a waste of human and financial resources that force up the cost of transaction. Such deficiencies even provide opportunities for private brokers to make illegal profits. Second, due to segmentation of the market, financial institutions lose many financial opportunities thus slowing down capital turnover and reducing mobility.

(2) Generally, the maturity of inter-bank lending tends to be too long with most of the activities aimed at expanding loans instead of accommodating liquidity needs. According to 'Information of Inter-bank Lending' in the Financial News of 16 July 1987, the maximum maturity of inter-bank lending can be as long as twelve months. Most terms are between two to three months and very few less than ten days. The 1989 *Almanac of China's Finance and Banking* reveals that of the total inter-bank lending in 1988, 27 per cent had a maturity of more than four months, 36.6 per cent between one to four months and 36.4 per cent less than one month. One obvious reason for this is that the banks borrow money with the principal aim of using the funds to extend loans to their client enterprises, and do not use it to replenish their inadequate reserves in the accounts of the central bank or imbalances in their bill clearing settlements.

The more fundamental reasons for the banks' behaviour are, first, with the absence of the risk of bankruptcy, defaults between financial institutions are frequent and consequently replenishing liquidity does not provide any incentives for inter-bank borrowing. On the contrary, local bank branches are keen to expand credit. Second, shortage of capital is universal in all enterprises throughout the country, as demand for investment to expand production and initiate new projects is extremely strong. Thus, there is a preference in demand for longer maturity bank loans. In such circumstances, inter-bank borrowings without adequate control over maturity are bound to induce banks to finance fixed investments outside the state plan, without consideration of the consequences. Even when maturity control was later imposed, due to weakness of other controls, the same practice by banks continued in some localities through covert use of funds and the automatic extension of the maturity of short-term financing. The expansion of fixed investments outside the state plan fuelled by such practices has caused many problems for the implementation of the state macroeconomic policy. Upon further analysis, these problems are also related to such problems as the enterprise system and the price of funds.

(3) Another unique phenomenon of China's inter-bank market is the unrestrained borrowing by participants. Inter-bank borrowings are used not only for ironing out fluctuations in liquidity, but also as an important instrument of bank liability management, which is the normal practice in foreign financial markets. In China, however, the amount of borrowing from the inter-bank market is substantial, sometimes several times as much as the level of deposits. There are several reasons. First, financial institutions in China are not managed as enterprises and therefore run no risk of bankruptcy. Second, inter-bank borrowing is not subject to reserve requirement of the central bank. Third, financial institutions are often forced to borrow substantially from non-local inter-bank markets in order to satisfy the demand for loans of enterprises. Such unrestrained borrowing is detrimental to the payment function of banks, especially when money is tight or when households or enterprises run on banks, or when borrowing enterprises are unable to repay on maturity (considering that assets of financial institutions are not diversified). In such cases payment and liquidity crises and cross-defaults are likely, which result in a chain reaction leading to chaos in the financial order of the country.

(4) The scale of the inter-bank market is parallel to the changes in the tightness of monetary policy of the central bank. With a relatively mature market mechanism, changes in monetary conditions are not necessarily accompanied by expansion or contraction of the inter-bank market because they can be accommodated either by changes in the level of interest rate in the inter-bank market or by structural changes in the financial market as a whole. China's experience over the past six years, however, has shown different characteristics. For instance, in 1986 when monetary conditions were relaxed, an intention to lend 100 million yuan was posted in one market for three weeks with no transaction taking place. In the

fourth quarter of 1989 when money was tightened, inter-bank market activities throughout the country almost ceased.

The reason for this phenomenon lies in the fact that when monetary policy is relaxed, the financial institutions borrow from the central bank at lower rates instead of going to the inter-bank market with its higher rates. When money is tightened, the reduction in money supply and the thin structure of the markets cause inter-bank activities to contract. In addition, during a period of tight monetary conditions, those banks with idle funds are not willing to lend to other financial institutions in case they are unable to make due repayments and the banks are left powerless to do anything about it. Having idle funds only means a reduction in earnings which in China is not the major concern of the management of banks. With such an operating mechanism, the size of the market will expand and contract together with changes in the conditions of the demand and supply of money.

The appearance of the above phenomena and the consequent problems are due to various complex reasons that can be summarised as follows. First, as financial markets are developed to enable the use of the market mechanism in the allocation of financial resources, China's financial institutions are only partly motivated by gaining profit. These financial institutions have not completely achieved the status of operational autonomy nor are they responsible for risks. They do not have to worry about losses, the cost of transactions, or having idle funds. Second, other short-term money market instruments have not been developed as they should be while the inter-bank market is being developed, thus forcing short-term investment activities of enterprises and financial institutions to rely solely upon inter-bank market activities as a substitute. Third, the economic system as a whole has not been able to provide an environment in which the inter-bank market is able to perform efficiently. Governments at different levels all intervene in financial activities, requiring banks to borrow more from other localities and lend less. Enterprises, however, always encourage banks to borrow long term in the inter-bank market for investments.

3 PROSPECTS FOR DEVELOPMENT

The above phenomena and problems are but minor aspects of the six years of development of China's inter-bank market. Generally speaking, the development of the inter-bank market is an innovation. A correct appraisal and analysis of the above problems is in the interest of improving and developing the market. My personal view is that the market should be developed in the following directions.

First, continuous efforts should be made to further reform and improve the country's economic and financial systems; otherwise, healthy development not only of the inter-bank market but also of the financial market as a whole cannot be achieved.

Second, if the inter-bank market is to have any dynamic development, then steps to bring about the enterprisation of bank management must be quickened. If bank management has little interest in profits and is not under much pressure of risk, then even the best form of market organisation would find it difficult to expand activities and broaden its scope. This applies not only to the inter-bank market, but also to other parts of the financial market. This is an important lesson from the experience of reform of China's financial system.

Third, there must be a strengthening of the regulation and development of the inter-bank market. This will be extremely difficult and will take a long time. Consequently, under the present economic system, it is especially important to strengthen the management of the market itself. This step has two aspects.

(1) Taking into account the characteristics of the economic and financial systems, appropriate rules and regulations should be formulated so as to ensure that the performance of the market is favourable for the achievement of macroeconomic policy objectives. The rules and regulations should include stipulations on the amount of borrowing and lending as well as transaction procedures, maturities, interest rates, the use of funds and provisions for examination and penalties by market authorities. For this reason the People's Bank of China has recently stipulated that inter-bank borrowing can only be used to accommodate balance of settlements and needs for working capital. It is forbidden to make fixed asset loans out of inter-bank borrowings. At present the maturity of inter-bank borrowing is generally stipulated to be within one month, and not more than four months for other financial institutions. It is also stipulated that the average balance of inter-bank borrowing from banks by financial institutions cannot exceed 5 per cent of the balance of deposits at the end of the previous month. For urban credit co-operatives, the ratio of borrowing balance to

equity capital is a maximum of 2:1. For other financial institutions, borrowing balance on average cannot exceed· their equity capital.

(2) There is a lack of communication between the 'markets', the 'centres' and the 'networks'. It should be reversed as soon as possible by building networks which connect all the markets, thus creating conditions for the quick dissemination of market information and for the formation ·of a unified market so as to boost the volume of transaction and lower the cost of financing. Meanwhile, a positive and analytical approach should be adopted to review the experience of the financial companies that were wound up, so that lessons can be drawn both from the way these companies were approved and how they were controlled and managed. Regulations governing financial companies should be formulated accordingly, specifying strict limits on their management principles and operational modes. Considering the vastness of China, five or six major cities should be selected for the establishment of companies (at the same time making sure to avoid duplication of markets in the same city or the same province) which can handle on a nationwide basis inter-bank activities, acceptance and trading of commercial bills of exchange, as well as the underwriting and trading of CDs and CPs. Such efforts, it is hoped, will link together smaller markets scattered around the country and promote the development of a unified money market in the country.

I believe that if the above can be effected, especially in the near term, and if regulation and development of the inter-bank network is strengthened, then the inter-bank market could be rapidly developed, notwithstanding difficulties in other areas of the financial market. Thus, it could still play a positive role in optimising the allocation of the financial resources of the country.

Notes

1 Business time was once a week or every ten days. Later, some places began operating daily.
2 Statistics used in this chapter are taken from the *Almanac of China's Finance and Banking*, various issues.

5

CHINA'S FINANCIAL INSTITUTIONS

Wu Xiaoling

In 1979 China began its reform of the economic system. The highly centralised Chinese economy began a gradual transition towards a planned socialist commodity economy. In the wake of this, the financial institutions which are indispensable to a commodity economy also underwent great changes. Of the socialist countries, China was among the first to establish a central bank system.

Prior to 1979, China's financial institutions consisted only of the People's Bank of China which handled industrial and commercial credit, savings and distribution of currency, the Bank of China which handled foreign currency, the People's Construction Bank of China which handled funds for capital construction and the People's Insurance Company of China which handled insurance for foreigners. These financial institutions were not run on a profit or loss basis, their funding came from the national budget, their operations were stipulated by the government and thus they were not banks in the real sense of the word, but simply state institutions to receive and pay out money.

After 1979, one by one, the Bank of China, the People's Construction Bank of China and the Insurance Company became independent economic bodies under the direct leadership of the State Council. Later, the Agricultural Bank of China, the Industrial and Commercial Bank of China, the Bank of Communications, the China International Trust and Investment Corporation, the China New Technologies Investment Company and other financial institutions were established. From 1 January 1984 the People's Bank of China ceased to handle general industrial and commercial credit and savings and became the Central Bank of China.

Over the past ten years, apart from financial institutions estab-

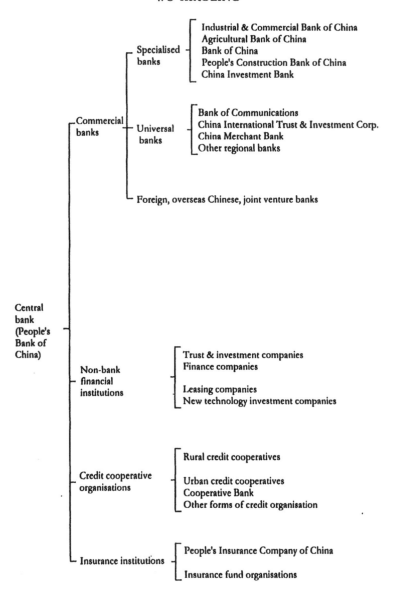

Figure 5.1 China's financial institutions

lished with state capital, other financial organisations have been set up. These include financial trust companies, negotiable securities companies and financial companies funded by local government and enterprises. There are also rural credit co-operatives funded through equity shares by farmers, and urban credit co-operatives funded by private entrepreneurs in the towns, by collective enterprises and even state units. Figure 5.1 presents a schematic structure of China's financial system. By the end of 1990, China had more than 181,000 financial institutions, with the state specialised banks as the mainstay under the leadership of the central bank.

1 THE REFORM OF CHINA'S FINANCIAL INSTITUTIONS

China's financial institutions have undergone many important changes since the reform.

1.1 China's financial institutions now have autonomy in the utilisation of funds

Prior to the reform, all domestic credit transactions were handled through the People's Bank of China. Branches of the People's Bank had no autonomy in granting credit. The People's Bank handed down through the credit plan for the branches the sum total of credit, as well as plans for credits according to items. Industrial credit, commercial credit and agricultural credit all had specific quotas. No adjustment or exchange between the various quotas were allowed, earmarked funds were to be used for stipulated purposes. The head office's management of its branches was extremely rigid.

After the People's Bank of China became the central bank in 1984 it strictly delineated its financial relationship with the various specialised banks. A deposit reserve system was established. The specialised banks under the new management system developed business mainly by relying upon their own ability to attract savings, and when there were insufficient deposits they could borrow from the People's Bank. Every year the People's Bank would hand down its lending quota on fixed assets to the specialised banks, and within these limits any extra deposits they received would allow them to extend additional loans. The People's Bank did not make any rules regarding the direction of loans and within the scale announced in its annual credit policy the specialised banks had autonomy in the utilisation of funds.

1.2 China's financial institutions have begun to have the right to open up new areas of business

Prior to 1979 the business scope of China's financial institutions was rigidly constrained. Their methods of raising and utilising funds were extremely simple: there were only two types of transaction, deposits and credit. Insurance was only for foreign transactions: there was no domestic market. Conventional commercial credits were always regarded as something incompatible with state planning and therefore forbidden. Consequently, banks did not have any business in the acceptance and discounting of commercial bills. Shares and bonds were considered as emanating from capitalism and were banned, and even using the name of the state to borrow funds both domestically and internationally was considered a type of insult, an expression of economic weakness, and could not be practised. As an expression of its economic strength, China once proudly proclaimed that it was the only country in the world that had neither foreign nor domestic debt.

The economic reform of 1979 made many people realise that finance was one means of developing a commodity economy, and that it does not carry with it the mark of ideology. China is in the preliminary stage of socialist development, and in the process of developing commodity production, finance becomes absolutely essential. Under the guidance of the state plan, as long as we strengthen the law and management, all forms of finance that are beneficial to developing commodity production may be used. This conceptual breakthrough, coupled with the autonomy of the banks in the utilisation of capital, has pushed China's financial institutions to continuously broaden their scope of business.

China's state banks have broken through the former rigid division of labour and begun to compete directly in their business activities. The Bank of China is no longer restricted to foreign exchange business, it has begun to handle loans in foreign exchange and in the depositing and lending of domestic currency. The Industrial and Commercial Bank of China is no longer confined to cities within China and has begun to extend into the vast countryside and abroad. The Agricultural Bank of China is no longer restricted to the countryside or to agriculture and it has entered cities and townships, and invested funds in industrial and commercial enterprises, particularly in rural enterprises. Apart from handling budgetary grants and lending relating to the reform scheme to substitute bank credit for budgetary grants, the People's Construction Bank of China is actively seeking deposits and extending medium- and long-term loans of a commercial nature.

China's various financial institutions have already gone beyond merely extending short-term loans and have entered the arena of medium- and long-term loans. As bank customers, China's enterprises have now acquired more freedom. They may choose the bank to handle their deposits, loans and accounts. Some enterprises even have accounts with a number of different banks to handle their deposits and loans. To an extent, the banks no longer have the obligation to open accounts for enterprises and give them loans; they may select the enterprises they want as clientele. Gradually the situation is becoming a competitive one where enterprises are choosing their banks and the banks selecting the enterprises, thus breaking down the monopolistic form of one enterprise to one bank.

With the overlapping of activities and the development of competition among banks, Chinese financial institutions continue to provide new services and products to attract clientele to increase deposits. In January 1982, Rong Yiren set up the China International Trust and Investment Corporation (CITIC) and was the first to go to Tokyo to raise capital by issuing private bonds to the sum of 10 billion Japanese yen, for a major project to build a large-scale chemical-fibre plant at Yizheng. Issuing bonds to raise funds became acceptable.

By December 1988 China's financial institutions had issued bonds abroad amounting to 480 billion Japanese yen, 1.5 billion US dollars, 0.8 billion West German marks and 0.7 billion Hong Kong dollars. In 1985 China's financial institutions began to issue domestic financial bonds with interest rates higher than the bank deposit rates for the same period. Such bonds could also be traded through the Bank of Communications. After this the Bank of China began to handle transferable certificates of fixed deposits of *renminbi*, aimed both at organisations and individuals. The rates of interest of the deposit certificates varied with the amount deposited and were set higher than the interest rate of bank deposits for the same period (Table 5.1).

Since the reforms and open door policy, commercial credit has

Table 5.1 Interest rates of certificates of deposit, 1990

	Amount (yuan)	Interest rate (percentage of bank interest rate for comparable maturity)
For individuals	500	105
	1,000	110
	3,000	115
	5,000	120
For organisations	100,000	105
	500,000	110
	1,000,000	115
	5,000,000	120

become accepted and developed. The banks have begun to handle the acceptance and discounting of commercial bills. On this basis the central bank also established re-discounting and re-financing facilities. Up till the end of 1988, specialised banks' discounting transactions amounted to 2.19 billion yuan, the People's Bank's re-discounting facilities handled 0.668 billion yuan. Although the amounts concerned were not large, none the less they revealed the direction of reform.

Apart from new business developed by the state specialised banks, many new non-bank financial institutions have appeared since the reform. They include trust and investment companies, leasing companies, securities companies and so on, all of which have developed rather quickly. They handle conventional financial business, and the relative importance of their activities in the financial system continues to grow. By the end of 1988 the amount of credit granted by the state banks amounted to 79.5 per cent of the national total, compared with 91.1 per cent in 1978. The proportion of credits granted by the trust and investment companies has developed from nothing in 1978 to 5.89 per cent in 1988. Since treasury bonds were first issued in 1981, various kinds of securities have been issued to raise capital amounting to 45 billion yuan by 1990. In July 1988 the state approved the trading of treasury bonds in seven cities – Shanghai, Shenyang, Chongqing, Wuhan, Guangzhou, Harbin and Shenzhen. These localities have subsequently set up securities companies engaged in the issuing, buying and selling of bonds. By the end of 1990 there were altogether some forty-four securities companies, 200 investment and trust companies that dealt in securities and 1,050 shop-fronts for securities trading.

1.3 The right of financial institutions to set interest rates, within a defined range, created conditions to use interest rates as a lever to adjust the economy

Prior to 1979, China had never attached importance to the role played by interest rates. During the Cultural Revolution it was considered that to obtain interest on deposits was a kind of exploitation and there were those who wanted to abolish paying interest on savings. It was only later when Premier Zhou Enlai intervened that the proposed abolition did not proceed. After the reform, China gradually came to attach importance to the role of interest rates and continues to carry out reform in this field:

1 The overall level of interest rates was raised. The interest rate for a one-year fixed saving deposit was raised from 3.24 per cent in 1978 to 13.14 per cent by 1990.

2 The interest rate structure has been rationalised so that rates are basically set according to the cost, terms and risk. Prior to August 1985 the interest rate for one-year loans was 7.82 per cent per annum, while the interest rate on fixed asset loans from one to three years was 5.76 per cent, and from five to ten years the rate was only 6.47 per cent. After August 1985 the interest rates for medium- and long-term loans were raised to a higher level than short-term loans.

3 The various financial institutions now have the authority to set their interest rates within a 30 per cent band above and below the base rate stipulated by the state. They have used this flexibility to attract deposits and adjust loans. In 1987 the Industrial and Commercial Bank of China developed a progressive interest rate scheme for its financial bonds. The annual rate for the bonds for the first year was 9 per cent (at the time the one-year bank savings deposit rate was 7.2 per cent, for five-year deposits it was 9.36 per cent), for the second year the interest rate was 10 per cent per annum, for the third year it was 11 per cent per annum, for the fourth year 12 per cent per annum and 13 per cent for the fifth year. The average interest rate was 10 per cent, and it did not surpass the permitted level of fluctuation stipulated by the People's Bank of China. However, this seem-

ingly very high progressive interest rate scheme proved very attractive to clients. After one year the principal capital and interest could at any time be redeemed, but no interest would be paid for the remaining years. The banks played up to the clients' desire for high interest rates and their unwillingness to lose any revenue in interest rates, and in a bond market yet undeveloped, they have found a comparatively good balance where the bonds provide a definite time of stability and liquidity, thus creating conditions for the smooth circulation of financial bonds.

In order to encourage enterprises to economise on the utilisation of funds, the specialised banks have adopted different interest rates for different enterprises. The specialised banks have audited and determined with their clients their credit limit and set them the task of speeding up capital turnover. For those enterprises which can decrease the amount of demand for credit, and surpass and complete the task of speeding up capital turnover, the specialised banks provide preferential rates of interest to loans, at a discount of 10–30 per cent below the stipulated interest rate of the state. If the amount of capital used by an enterprise is high, then the task of speeding up capital turnover cannot be completed, and the banks then charge a premium of 10–30 per cent on the interest rate for their loans.

1.4 China's financial institutions are carrying out corporate management and have gained some autonomy in their own finance, personnel and in setting up branches and subsidiaries

Prior to 1981 China's banks worked within the budget system, and bank profits were all handed over to the Ministry of Finance. Every year the Ministry allotted a certain amount as credit funds (in some years of financial difficulty no funds were allocated). The recurrent expenditure of banks to make payroll, and every item of expenditure, is rigidly stipulated by the state.

After 1981, China's financial institutions adopted a system of profit retention. The Ministry of Finance ruled what could be counted as operating costs. An agreed retention rate of after-tax profits is reached for each specialised bank, and after paying business tax, an agreed proportion of the profits is left to the banks (the proportion for the various specialised banks varies) as their own funds. Of the non-retained profits, 62 per cent should be remitted to the Ministry of Finance, 38 per cent should be left to the banks as credit funds. Credit funds are state funds and the banks may only use these for loans, not for other purposes. The after-tax profit retained by the banks should be used to develop business and to fund employee welfare and bonuses.

Prior to the reform, the banks practised a highly centralised method of management. Bank branches had no autonomy with regard to personnel, financial affairs and business operation. After the reform, the vitality of the local banks increased. Specialised banks have appropriately devolved their cost-accounting units. The provincial and city branches now have independent accounting, the right to appoint or dismiss cadres and the right to set up branches and subsidiaries. In giving branches the right to handle personnel, finance and business matters, the specialised banks have set up different forms of contract responsibility systems, so that the branches will shoulder responsibility and take risks.

2 EVALUATION OF REFORM TO CHINA'S FINANCIAL INSTITUTIONS

China's financial reforms have brought a great deal of dynamism to financial institutions and this has accompanied the process of developing a commodity economy. Finance has penetrated into all aspects of life, and is playing a bigger role in the national economy. In 1978, 79.1 per cent of the funds the state put into the economy came from budgetary grants, 20.9 per cent was provided by bank credit. By 1988 the amount of construction funding provided by the state budget went down to 36.8 per cent, while the amount provided by the banks increased to 63.4 per cent. In 1978, fixed assets investment by state enterprises and units all came from the state budget; by 1988 the funding from bank loans was 230 per cent of the budgetary grants. Apart from utilising bank credit, the government has begun to issue bonds to raise capital and by the end of 1989, the government had issued a total of 120 billion yuan in treasury bonds and other public bonds.

The establishment of specialised banks, the setting up of different kinds of financial institutions and the enlargement of the autonomy of financial enterprises have stimulated the initiative of financial institutions to compete for deposits, enlarge their lending and other financial business, and has increased the process of monetisation of the national economy. China's financial institutions have increased in number from 100,000 in 1981 to 181,000 by the end of 1990. Between 1978–90 China's money supply M_3 (all bank deposits plus currency in circulation) increased at an annual average rate of over 20 per cent. The ratio of M_3 to national income increased from 44.7 per cent to 87 per cent. The rapid development of China's rural enterprises has been supported by the banks and credit co-operatives. The reliance of all enterprises on the banks has greatly increased, so the cyclic tightening and relaxing of bank credit can have an enormous effect on their activities. Finance is just coming out from being an appendage to the Ministry of Finance to being as important as it is, a means of adjusting national economic policy.

However, these ten years of reforms leave much to be desired and urgently need further improvement. First, China's financial institutions, especially the specialised state banks, have no means of breaking away from administrative interference, and they cannot extricate themselves from the position of guaranteeing provision of capital for enterprises. They have little room to manoeuvre in the autonomous usage of capital, and they have difficulty in enhancing its profitable use and raising its social and economic effectiveness.

Exercising direct control over economic construction by the government is the main feature of a planned economic state. In line with the progress made in reform to the economic system over recent years at all levels, government in China has gradually relaxed direct control over the economy. It is beginning to use credit, interest rates, tax revenue, prices and other economic levers to guide enterprises and markets. However, the main components of the national economy are still directly controlled by the government. Increases in output, the value of industry and agriculture, the speed of economic development and social construction are still the main criteria for judging whether a government or a regional government has done its work well. Economic construction needs capital funds and when finance is insufficient, attention is focused on the banks. In such a situation the banks cannot avoid government interference.

The specialised banks were established according to administrative areas, so that they correspond with each tier of government. Despite efforts over recent years to strengthen the independence of the banks, the cadres at each level are appointed by the head office and its higher-level branches, so as to affect a vertical leadership within the banking system. However, the Party and Youth League affiliations of these cadres still rest with the local regions. The cadres of the various financial institutions are subject to arrangements by local government for the supply of their food, clothing, shelter and transportation. This means that the interest of the banks at different levels is closely linked to the interests of the locality. The banks are therefore willing to do their best to serve the interests of the local government.

For decades the banks of China have been an important part of the state bureaucracy. Even after the reform, the specialised banks are treated by many people only as special enterprises which conduct business in money and credit. Banks assume a dual role. On the one hand, they must function as a commercial financial institution. On the other hand, they have to facilitate macroeconomic control and adjustment. This dual role imposes on the specialised banks a responsibility to complete the assignments given them by the state. Spurred by this self-interest and sense of responsibility, specialised banks have no way of resisting the interference of the various tiers of government, thus they have very little leeway to exercise their rights in the utilisation of funds.

The state enterprises of China are important clients of the specialised banks: over 90 per cent of the funds of the specialised banks is channelled to state enterprises. However, China's state enterprises are not real independent producers. Some of them are enterprises that only take profit but not the responsibility for loss. When the enterprise is running at a profit it collects various kinds of funds for welfare and bonuses and raises wages, but when the enterprise is losing or it cannot pay its bills, the state, for the sake of social stability, will not allow it to be declared bankrupt. Consequently, when the enterprise has no means of repaying its bank loans, the bank has no other choice but to give additional credit to save the enterprise. The state-owned status of the specialised banks makes people feel that the banks and the enterprises are one, all state organisations, that they should give support and help to each other, and that the banks have a duty to supply capital to state enterprises. In such an environment it is very difficult for the banks to have any autonomy over the flow of credit.

The administrative interference by the government and the reliance of enterprises on the banks mean that the social and economic efficiency of capital is not high. In terms of attaining an overall balance of the national economy, the specialised banks know that the construction of some processing enterprises and the importation of some production lines are not appropriate, that they will create a situation where productive capacity far outstrips the supply of inputs and raw materials, where market supply exceeds demand, where imported equipment and technology are duplicated and investments are made blindly. However, for the interests of the region, and under local government pressure, the banks have to provide funds to such projects.

Moreover, for the sake of the region's economic growth, and to solve the local employment problem, the banks must still give loans to local enterprises that are not economically viable, operating at a loss, although it is known they have neither future prospects nor ability to repay their loans. This type of finance has caused over-expansion, and led to the irrational deployment of resources, contributing to the decline in economic profitability.

Of the newly established financial institutions during reform, the local trust and investment companies all have a rather strong regional flavour. Their main task is to raise funds for local government and local projects. This has helped promote local economic prosperity. However, it has accelerated China's investment inflation, and aggravated the problems of excess social demand over supply.

Second, specialised banks now have a certain degree of operational autonomy, but they still do not assume complete economic responsibility for business risks. This has facilitated the trend of blind competition and blind expansion. This makes it difficult for the central bank to pursue the intended policy aim of economic control. It has forced the central bank to revert to direct control, thus reducing the flexibility as well as the profitability of its fund utilisation.

Since the establishment of the system of profit retention and a lending policy based on direct linkage between deposit and loan, the bonuses and welfare of bank employees are directly tied to the business performance of the bank, and the banks have been very energetic in attracting deposits and expanding credit. Many banks have an extensive network of subsidiaries set up in townships and rural areas, using every means to attract customers, extend loans and develop strong competition. This, of course, has furthered the development of financial services, but it has inevitably given rise to the improper establishment of some subsidiaries, the contravening of finance regulations and the granting of inappropriate loans. The state-owned specialised banks represent the state. In the eyes of the people even the urban or rural credit co-operatives are part of the state banks.

When a financial institution mismanages, resulting in serious losses, the head office and the local government will not close it down, but will find ways and means of subsidising it. Some institutions have extended large loans with very poor results, so that they have such a low level of liquidity that they cannot cope with withdrawals of deposits. In order to protect the prestige of the state and social stability, the upper-level bank branches and the local People's Bank will transfer money from other parts of the country, or the People's Bank will extend loans to keep up appearances. This way of doing things aids the blind expansionist behaviour of the local banks.

Specialised banks are supposed to be state banks, but with the interference of local governments and in pursuit of their own economic interests they invariably use their limited funds to guarantee the economic needs of the local region. Therefore, when funds are needed to procure products to meet central government's export targets, when agricultural and side-line products need to be purchased and important projects need to be guaranteed, and when central government enterprises need funds, and when credit funds are not available, thus forcing the central bank to create and supply base money and expand the volume of credit. In 1984 this caused total bank loans to exceed their planned level by over 100 per cent, and in 1986 the credit plan was exceeded by 75 per cent. When it proved difficult to constrain the specialised banks by economic means, the central bank strengthened its use of administrative measures.

After 1987, in order to strengthen control over finance, the People's Bank of China imposed credit ceilings and set up loan quota control for fixed capital investments, for rural and country town enterprise loans for agricultural and side-line products. This type of control has strengthened macroeconomic management, but greatly decreased flexibility in the utilisation of funds. For instance, in some regions the specialised banks have excess reserves in the central bank, but they do not have a credit loan quota, so they cannot extend loans. Some regional specialised banks have a credit loan quota but no excess reserves in the central bank, and they cannot extend loans. Over the past few years, financial institutions have developed the inter-bank market, but this can only ease temporary illiquidity. It is not geared to solving the problem of mismatching in the distribution of base money and loan quotas. Obstructed by the seeking of regional interests, it is difficult to re-allocate liquidity and lending quotas among regions. The efficient utilisation of funds is therefore lowered.

Third, under an irrational price and interest rate system, the specialised banks' pursuit of self-interest results in funds being invested in projects which are not compatible with the interests of the whole society, thus reducing the role of finance in the optimisation of resource allocation.

When prices correctly signal the value of commodities and the demands of society, when interest rates can basically reflect the cost of capital usage and when everybody can shoulder risks, profit-seeking banks can ensure that money goes into the development of those businesses on which society places a high priority. However, decades of a planning system in China have resulted in the price of many commodities seriously deviating from value and social demand. There is a wide disparity between the rate of return (including tax) on capital among industries.

In 1982, the rate of return (and tax) on capital for industrial enterprises was 23.5 per cent, for light industry it was 46.3 per cent, for heavy industry it was 16.8 per cent. This disparity in the rate of return and tax on capital, coupled with the fiscal contract responsibility system for regional governments, has caused funds to pour into light industry. While this has stimulated the development of light industry, bringing about an abundance of consumer goods, it also aggravates the shortage of raw materials and energy. It has brought about the 'silk war', the 'cotton war' and the 'wool war', with people competing to buy various agricultural and side-line products, thus pushing prices up and creating imbalances in the economic structure.

In order to support selected industries, the Chinese government has put into practice a system of preferential rates of interest. By the end of 1984 there were forty-seven kinds of preferential rates of interest, which accounted for around 90 per cent of all per-mitted types and levels of loan interest rates. The establishment of preferential rates was intended to provide capital at low prices to develop industries. However, some of the preferential rates of interest produce income lower than the cost to the banks of attracting deposits. By extending preferential loans, not only do the banks reduce revenue, it also means they have to sustain losses. For instance, miscellaneous consumption goods are necessary for people's livelihood, but their prices and returns are low, and enterprises do not like to produce them. The state fears that a raising of the prices of these goods might affect the livelihood of the people, so in November 1982 the Chinese government stipulated preferential loans to enterprises producing such items at a monthly rate of 4.8 per cent. In comparison, the normal bank loan rate at the time was 6 per cent, and the annual deposit rate was 6 per cent. Other than being ordered to do so, banks would normally not extend such loans.

After 1984, the Chinese government began gradually to carry out price reform and tidy up the interest rate structure. In 1988, the average annual rate of return to capital in industrial enterprises was 20.5 per cent, in light industry it was 26.91 per cent, in heavy industry it was 17.25 per cent: the difference in the rates between the various industries was shrinking. The state has also begun to adjust the preferential rates of interest. At present, apart from national minority regions and welfare factories of civil administration departments, all other preferential credit now takes the form of interest subsidies. Now whoever wants to give preferential interest rates must also fund the required interest subsidies. Such measures have improved external conditions for the enterprisation of the specialised banks. However, under the present price system, allowing the banks to pursue their vested interest will not result in capital flowing to where society needs it. Therefore, administrative interference becomes necessary, thus decreasing the role of finance in the optimisation of resource allocation.

3 TRENDS IN THE DEVELOPMENT OF CHINA'S FINANCIAL INSTITUTIONS

The above-mentioned problems in China's financial institutions during the reform are commonly acknowledged. They have caused a renewal of the controversy over the direction of reform of China's financial institutions. This controversy has existed since the beginning of the reform, and in the face of China's urgent economic difficulties it is the focus of rethinking. A major controversy over the direction of reform to China's financial institutions is about the nature of the state's specialised banks. The issue is whether China's specialised banks should operate solely as enterprises, or as institutions with a dual responsibility as enterprises with responsibilities in public administration.

One point of view considers that China's banking system does not have the characteristics of the capitalist system, but is an inevitable product of the commodity economy. If China is to develop a socialist planned commodity economy, then it must establish an appropriate and compatible central bank system. Under a central bank system, China's specialised banks are state-owned enterprises and they *cannot* at the same time have the responsibility for macroeconomic control. If the state specialised banks really become enterprises and develop fair competition between them, then they can pursue the profit motive and under external pressure correctly deal with relations between financial mobility, security and profitability, and work hard to raise the efficiency of capital. If they operate as an enterprise, then the specialised banks can establish an equal co-operative relationship with enterprises, will not lord it over them and will not underwrite the provision of capital to enterprises. By being an enterprise, paying attention to economic efficiency and to business reputation, the state specialised banks will be able to open up new business and to respond appropriately to the indirect control measures of the central bank (deposit reserve ratio, re-discount rate).

It is only by becoming an enterprise that the specialised banks can develop new ways of raising funds and creating different kinds of financial instruments. It is only when financial institutions are diversified that a financial market can come into being. With financial markets, the efficiency of capital utilisation can be raised, capital mobility promoted and resource allocation optimised.

China's economy is a planned commodity economy. The socialist nature of the economy is based on predominant public ownership. The planned nature of the economy is manifested in the central bank system by two aspects. One is the formation of state-owned specialised financial institutions which are engaged in financial matters of a policy nature, which are allowed to extend loans for the basic development of the national economy such as the infrastructure and important projects. These institutions take the aims of the government as their responsibility, their objective is not to make profits. The second aspect is that the central bank proclaims its credit policy each year, and directs the state-owned financial institutions in their financial investments.

However, at present China's price system has still not been rationalised, state enterprises have still not become real enterprises, the social security system has not been completely established, new market organisations are yet to be formed. Consequently, conditions for the enterprisation of financial institutions are still not met. The state specialised banks can only practise corporate management, and gradually create conditions for branches below the provincial level to become real enterprises.

Another viewpoint considers that China's economic system is a planned economy, integrated with the market as a regulator. Under such a system, the central bank and the specialised banks are all state banks, and all have functions in macroeconomic adjustment. Only the division of labour is different. Specialised banks raise funds in different areas to satisfy the need of the state plan. The central bank, apart from using economic means to exercise control over the specialised banks, uses even more administrative measures and maintains guidance and control over the banks by imposing credit ceilings and targets.

In this context, specialised banks must clarify their division of labour and must concentrate on serving their assigned sector. They must not go in for diversified business. All financial institutions must be completely reviewed, all non-bank financial institutions should be abolished, the subsidiaries and branches of the specialised banks should be streamlined, competition should not be advocated among financial institutions. The reason why there is financial chaos is due to competition. Enterprises must be forbidden to have accounts in many banks, and the supervisory role of the banks over the enterprises should be strengthened, so as to raise the efficiency of utilisation of funds. The development of shares, bonds and commercial credit should be strictly controlled, and control by the banks over the volume of credit should be strengthened.

The trend of reform of China's financial institutions still has to be explored in practice. On two points there is common agreement. First, the socialist direction of China's economy will not change. Private management of China's finance industry will not be permitted, public ownership will be maintained and not change. Second, China's financial institutions cannot return to the past with the system of one big bank. It is within these premisses that one must explore a new financial system that is suitable to Chinese conditions and commodity production.

References

1 *Almanac of China's Finance and Banking*, various issues.
2 Liu Hongru (ed.) (1988) *Studies of the Problems of Reform of China's Financial System* (Beijing: Chinese Financial Press).
3 *Statistical Yearbook of China*, various issues.
4 Xu Yulong (ed.) (1988) *Yinhang Jiyehua (Enterprisation of Banks)* (Beijing: Jingji Guangli Chubanshe).

6

ISSUES IN THE REFORM OF CHINA'S RURAL FINANCIAL SYSTEM

Huang Yanxin

In establishing a socialist market economy, it is imperative to further develop the goods market, but it is especially important to establish factor markets. For this reason, it is of great significance to establish a well-functioning financial system – a new rural financial system led by the government policy banks and developed together with state-owned commercial banks, joint stock commercial banks and other forms of co-operative bank.

1 THE ESTABLISHMENT OF A WELL-FUNCTIONING ORGANISATIONAL STRUCTURE FOR THE AGRICULTURAL DEVELOPMENT BANK OF CHINA

The financial system reform, an important element of the economic reform, has been implemented throughout the nation to meet the demand of establishing a socialist market economy. One of the tasks in this financial system reform is to establish a policy bank, such as the Agricultural Development Bank of China (ADBC). The newly established bank will, based on government credit policy, mobilise agricultural policy credit funds, take over the government agricultural policy-related financial businesses and play a fiscal role by allocating grants and credits to agriculture. That is to say that directed policy loans should be handled by the ADBC and be separated from the Agricultural Bank of China (ABC). This business segregation has a very positive and practical implication, whether it is to provide a better service to the rural financial system, to better implement government sectoral industry policies and regional development, to improve the efficiency of utilising government credit to ensure healthy rural development or to turn the 'ABC into an independent and profit-making commercial bank. For the establishment of the Agricultural Development Bank of China, a number of issues need to be considered:

1 The reality of the rural sector must be considered in building the organisational structure for the newly established ADBC. Policy loans usually involve large amounts of funds across many sectors and apply to every single county/city in the country. We should establish branches in all rural counties/townships and immediately start business operations with appropriate manpower. This is to ensure policy loans are used for genuine rural economic development and for agricultural procurement, so that the bank's role of contributing to progress in the development of rural production and farming can be made effective. If we only have branches in certain areas, other areas without branches will suffer unnecessarily in their rural economic development due to delays in the extension and use of policy loans.

2 The newly established ADBC and the old ABC differ in their business nature, tasks and operational goals. Because of these differences, all other specialised banks (Industrial and Commercial Bank of China, People's Construction Bank of China and the Bank of China) should hand over business relating to agricultural policy loans and fiscal funds for the support of the rural sector to the ADBC once it is established, rather than handing them over first to the former ABC, which would in turn hand them over some time in the future to the ADBC. This direct handing-over procedure should be closely followed, even if it means that the ADBC will be delayed in getting all the business of policy loans and fiscal funds from other specialised banks. As far as the relationship between the two banks is concerned, it is the ADBC that assigns the ABC as an agent to conduct policy loan business and not vice versa. In the event that a local branch of the ADBC cannot yet commence operations, its higher supervising level of the ADBC can commission a lower-level ABC branch to conduct these lending activities.

3 As a government policy bank, the ADBC is, from the nature and scope of its business activities, a special bank for carrying out the government's industry policy and assisting agricultural development. It has a very close relationship with the government administrative department responsible for agriculture. The government can, through this policy bank, exercise macroeconomic

132

control over the production and marketing of agricultural products to ensure stable agricultural development and rural prosperity. Therefore, it is necessary to clearly define the relationship between the ADBC and the Ministry of Agriculture.

On the basis of overseas experience, agricultural policy banks are mostly under the supervision of departments of agriculture. For example, the Finance Companies for Agricultural Products in the United States are under the Department of Agriculture. The Japanese Central Agricultural and Forestry Credit Bank is subordinate to Japan's Agriculture and Forestry Ministry. In China, while satisfying government credit policy requirements, the operations of the ADBC should be subject to the supervision of the Ministry of Agriculture because the implementation of the government's agricultural policy is the responsibility of the department. It is inappropriate for the ADBC to be directed by any other department, as it would create difficulty for the Ministry of Agriculture in implementing a unified and consistent agricultural policy.

4 The scope of agricultural policy loans should be properly defined. The production and circulation of agricultural products are integral parts of the accumulation and growth process. To ensure the efficient supply of agricultural products is not about how much agricultural goods the government purchases from producers, or how much the government is stockpiling those goods. Rather, it is about developing production and reaching an equilibrium between demand and supply. For this reason, it is more important to issue policy loans for supporting agricultural production than to extend loans to state-owned commercial enterprises for procuring agricultural products.

The establishment of the ADBC in China is a historical step in the transition to the employment of credits as a means to control and support agricultural production. However, this is not to deny that, at the time when the issue of policy loan utilisation was considered, state-owned commercial enterprises faced a severe shortage of funds and as a result, the problem of IOU (*Bai Tiao*) emerged when these enterprises issued IOUs to farmers in exchange for purchased goods. The purpose of establishing a policy bank seems to aim at solving this problem rather than to play a supportive role for agricultural production.

In the Articles of Association of the ADBC, instead of stating clearly that supporting agricultural production and meeting the needs of rural economic development comprise its lending policy, the main policy lending business is stated to be loans to meet the needs of state-owned commercial enterprises for agricultural procurement and stockpiling. Furthermore, appropriate credit funds have not been made available and transferred to the ADBC. The consequence is that sufficient funds cannot be allocated to the right spot, so these special policy loans cannot be extended and utilised where they ought to be. Appropriate increases in loans for supporting agricultural production, and switching part of the ADBC's procurement lending to loans for production, will have significant effects in supporting agricultural production and rural development and will speed up the reform of state-owned commercial enterprises.

2 REFORM OF THE RURAL CREDIT CO-OPERATIVES

Rural credit co-operatives (RCCs) are an important part of the Chinese financial system. At the end of 1992, there were 52,599 RCCs with independent accounting, among which 50,271 were at the township (*Xiang*) level, with 815 associated village credit co-operatives (*Lian Cun XingYong She*), 95 village-level credit co-operatives and 1,418 associated co-operative business outlets. There were 46,158 RCCs without independent accounting, among which there were 33,443 credit co-operative branches and 12,715 saving stations. In addition, there were 234,294 RCC agencies plus 2,249 unions of rural credit co-operatives.[1]

The rural credit co-operatives were established in the 1950s by gathering funds through issues of shares to farmers. For various reasons, they have become a financial institution run by government officials and have drifted away from serving directly the interests of farmers. Since the rural reform, the RCCs have made some progress in widening their scope of business, improving customer service and supporting rural economic development. However, little substantive achievement has been made in reaching their three fundamental goals (to have member involvement in their organisation, a democratic approach in management and flexibility in operation). RCCs have not played their role of being a truly co-operative financial institution co-operating with farmers as members. They have not realigned their relationship with member farmers. Consequently, the RCCs have become the main channel for the outflow of funds from the rural sector. At the end of 1992, the sum of RCC reserve and other deposits with the ABC reached 108.05 billion yuan, accounting for 44.3 per cent of RCC total assets.[2] At the end of December 1993, that sum reached 188.262 billion yuan.[3] This led to the enormous amount of funds flowing out of the countryside to the cities and from rural sectors to non-rural sectors. Now we should examine and re-assess this phenomenon and ask ourselves whether it is for the benefit of the development of the rural economy. To facilitate the development of the market economy in the rural sector and to meet the credit demands of the farmers, we should speed up the reform of the RCCs under the co-operative principle and implement the following measures.

2.1 RCCs should sever their dependent links with the ABC

At present, the state-run nature and bureaucratic management style of the RCCs have not changed. They are reflected in the following aspects:

RCCs are subordinate to and supervised by the ABC.
RCC senior managers are appointed by the government.
Member farmers of RCCs do not have rights to supervise or manage those activities of the RCCs from which they do not receive direct benefits.

In order to advance the reform process and establish a new rural financial system, RCCs must be run independently of the government financial system. The RCCs and the ABC are two different organisations in their characteristics, types of business activities and customers. To make the RCC a financial institution that truly incorporates the joint effort of member farmers, and in accordance with the government's decision on financial reform, this separation process must be carried out speedily to cut off totally the RCC's 'umbilical' relationship with the former ABC. This is especially important at the time of the establishment of the ADBC and during the ABC's transformation into a commercial bank. Otherwise it will worsen the problem of the already severe shortage of funds for the rural sector due to the continuous rural capital outflow, as the profit-maximising ABC will continue to channel funds to other sectors and industries with higher returns. This will severely hamper the development of the rural economy. After total separation from the ABC, the RCCs should operate autonomously, under the principle of adherance to relevant national credit policy and regulation and be responsible for their profits and losses.

2.2 Clear definition of ownership rights

For the RCC to function as a true co-operative financial institution, it is of fundamental importance to have clearly defined property rights. Only after that can we rationalise the relation between the RCCs and farmers and transform them from a state-run financial institution to a financial institution run by the people. The initial capital of the RCCs, as mentioned earlier, was made up of shares subscribed by member farmers. These shares should still belong to these founding farmers. The capital accumulated over the years by the RCCs should belong mostly to these founding member farmers, and can be taken account of by increasing appropriately the amount of their shares. However, these newly allotted shares should not be divided or withdrawn. They can only serve as a basis for the distribution of RCC benefits to members. Another part of the accumulated capital can be used as a contribution to establishing retirement and pension funds for RCC staff, with the remaining part contributing to the RCC's public accumulation.

2.3 Independent operation

In the process of reforming the RCCs, it should be made clear that RCCs at different levels are independent financial organisations. The relationship among them is neither that of government administrative hierarchical levels nor that of a company head office and its subsidiaries or branches. Rather, the relationship among them is based on the operational level RCCs, which forge joint cooperation level by level, from the bottom up, to establish associated co-operatives or unions. There should be equal competition in their business activities.

2.4 Democratic management style

As a co-operative financial organisation, there should be two-way freedom of choice between a RCC and its members. Farmers should have the freedom to choose whether they want to join or leave. They should also be free to join one or more RCCs. The principle of voluntary entry and exit must be upheld. Within the RCCs, there should be a democratic management system – one vote per household. It is also important to establish and improve the system of general members' meetings and to ensure its functionality. The Board of Directors and the Supervisory Committee should be elected by the member representatives' meeting. The business operation, financial accounts and major decisions should be reported to the member representatives' meeting so that members can monitor their performance.

2.5 Fair competition

In the new era of establishing a market economy, state-owned commercial banks and co-operative financial institutions should be made clearly aware that they are subject to market competition and are equal participants. The circumstance should not occur where types of credit activities and regions where these activities can proceed are artificially segregated by either state-owned commercial banks or co-operative financial institutions. Discriminatory policies towards the co-operative financial institutions should not be allowed. Only through competition can the state-owned commercial banks improve their management and provide better services.

Through the reform of the RCCs, two issues should be resolved. First, the existing problem of capital outflow from the countryside to the cities via the RCCs should be solved, and, second, the RCCs should provide a better service for the development of the rural economy and agricultural production. Only when these two issues are resolved can the reform of the RCCs be deemed a success.

After several years of reform, some RCCs are likely to develop into a co-operative financial institution with active participation by member farmers. Others will never be able to become such an institution. The latter can become state-owned commercial banks and discard the RCC name after dissolving and withdrawing all share subscriptions.

On the question of establishing a Rural Co-operative Bank (RCB), the reform agenda is to form county-level RCBs, on the basis of county-level Associated RCCs, with the participation of township-level Associated RCCs. My view is that, first, instead of all RCCs participating in forming a new RCB, we should build

RCBs on the basis of those RCCs that have been genuinely reformed and are now truly farmers' own financial institutions. Second, the newly formed RCB should not be a monopoly and competition must exist. That is to say, there should be many RCBs. Without competition, even if they are a co-operative bank, they will lose the concept of efficiency and will easily emerge as an independent rent-seeking entity that works against the interest of its co-operative partners. Besides, establishing RCBs under the principle of competition will enhance the central bank's effectiveness in its macro control of financial markets.

To deepen the reform of the financial system, it is necessary to separate financial institutions carrying out government policies from those financial institutions conducting commercial activities, and to allow the co-existence of different kinds of financial institutions with the commercial banks as the mainstream. Apart from establishing rural and urban co-operative banks, it is also necessary to set up a batch of joint stock commercial banks as an experiment.

3 SUPPORTING THE HEALTHY DEVELOPMENT OF THE RURAL CO-OPERATIVE FUND ASSOCIATIONS

Since the reform, a remarkable change in rural economic development is the rapid development of a new and enterprising financial institution – the Rural Cooperative Fund Association (RCFA). The RCFAs started from a process of clearing debts and turning debts into loans (*Qingcaishouqian, Yiqianzhuandai*). After adopting the household contract responsibility system, the management of funds on many collectives became confusing and problematic. Individual farmers owed the collectives increasing amounts of money. The problem of improper management, idle funds and poor utilisation of collective funds was becoming increasingly severe. Some collectives started to 'stock-take' their assets. They collected the debts owed to them by individuals and those which could not be collected were turned into loans. In order to manage these activities, administrative organisations were established. This was the initial impetus for the establishment of RCFAs. Their management structure is based on the principle that individuals' idle funds are managed by villages and villages' funds are managed by townships (*Xiang*). These institutions were born at a time when reform in the rural financial system is lagging behind. They arose because the existing system could not satisfy the needs of rural commercial and economic development and cannot respond to the funds requirements arising from rural marketisation and industrial restructuring. This is especially the case when scattered individual farmers have need of small amounts of short-term working capital for developing production for the market.

Farmers greatly welcome the arrival of the RCFAs, since they meet the need for increasing their production and income. Since 1984, when a few areas experimented with this concept, RCFAs have experienced rapid acceptance and growth in the country. According to the preliminary statistics provided by the Ministry of Agriculture, at the end of 1993 there were 128,400 RCFAs, among which there were 17,800 at the township level and 110,600 in the villages, accounting for 38 per cent of the total number of townships and 15 per cent of the total number of villages, gathering funds worth 20 billion yuan during the year. In the last three years, debts collected by the RCFAs amounted to 2 billion yuan. Of these funds, 94 per cent have been used to support the working capital needs of planting, animal husbandry, rural enterprises and provision of agricultural social goods and services. The establishment of the RCFAs alleviated farmers' problems of funds shortages for developing agricultural production and rural economy. Because the Associations also handed over the profits to the fund owners, they have increased farmers' income. From 1990 to 1992, the income received by farmers from the Associations reached 1.34 billion yuan.[4]

Not only have the RCFAs channelled idle funds to help solve the problem of fund shortage faced by farmers, they have also prevented money-lenders from charging high interest in the informal credit market, and have therefore reduced private lenders' activities by 30 per cent. However, several theoretical issues need to be addressed here regarding the further development of the Associations:

1 The RCFA is an important element in the development of the rural co-operative economy. This institution has the characteristics of the socialist co-operative economy and should not be rejected because it is the creation of farmers in response to the current market-economic development. The development of

RCFAs has demonstrated that both the scope and contents of rural economic co-operation have been enlarged and promoted.

2 The establishment of RCFAs provides effective competition to other financial institutions and has not disturbed and destabilised the financial market. Both the RCFAs and the original RCCs are co-operative financial institutions that belonged to the farmers. After the RCCs lost farmers' trust for reasons mentioned earlier, and after the failure of attempts to change them back to how they were originally intended, farmers went on to establish a financial institution of their own. The development of the RCFAs will have a positive effect on the reform of the RCCs. The co-existence of these two competitors will prevent either one from monopolising their business activities, and will also stimulate the provision of wider and better services to the development of the rural market economy.

Actively mobilising and channelling funds are the normal activities for RCFAs, and they are fundamentally different from creating instability in the financial market. In 1993, they mobilised funds of just over 20 billion yuan, which was not large enough to form any threat to the nation's financial market. The evidence indicated that the chaos in the financial market in 1993 was caused by the activities of state banks, including illegal inter-bank money-market transactions, speculation in real estate and participation in share trading. In the first half of 1993 alone, improper inter-bank lending between state specialised banks reached 100 billion yuan, equivalent to 19 per cent of the annual total lending for basic construction (517 billion yuan) by the state banking system. At the end of 1993, inter-bank money-lending between the specialised banks during the tightening of financial discipline amounted to more than 83 billion yuan.[5]

3 The RCFAs should be allowed to conduct deposit and lending activities under general government financial regulations and policy. Being a financial intermediary, operating such activities which comply with financial law and regulation is normal. One should not disallow RCFAs from engaging in deposit and lending activities simply because they are the initiative of farmers. If the RCCs are allowed to attract deposits and to lend, naturally the RCFAs should also be permitted to undertake these activities, since they serve the same function in facilitating rural economic development. If these activities are not allowed, the purpose of the existence of the RCFAs will be lost and the very

high interest loans in the informal credit market will inevitably and rapidly expand, which will be against the objective of the government's current rural policy.

4 The RCFAs should be a profit-making organisation. As a financial intermediary, its primary goal should be to raise economic efficiency. Otherwise, there will be no guarantee to farmers that funds they invest in RCFAs will produce any return. Farmers will not be attracted to participate as a member of an RCFA and those who are in it will want to withdraw their shares, making the existence of the Associations unsustainable. Therefore, on the basis of giving priority to the needs of agricultural production (especially Association members') and members' consumption demands, RCFAs must return a profit at an increasing rate.

5 There is a need to establish a well-functioning organisation for the RCFAs, and to set up proper systems and procedures for managing membership shares, auditing flows of funds, financial accounting and the distribution of profits. Staff training should be strengthened to raise the quality of services. Business operating procedures should be standardised and the channels for raising more funds be expanded in order to better service the needs of agricultural production and the development of the rural market economy. It must be stressed that the RCFAs should institutionalise the co-operative character of the organisation, and should not repeat the experience of the RCCs.

6 The RCFAs should adopt an effective system for risk management. As farmers own the Associations, the risk should be borne jointly by member farmers. With the increasing amount of funds handled by the RCFAs and the consequent expanded areas where these funds are used, it is inevitable that the problems of overdue and non-performing loans will emerge. The RCFAs should therefore set up risk reserve provision and proper insurance in a risk protection and guarantee system.

7 It is necessary to ensure the independence and autonomy of the Associations' business operation. Assistance from local government has provided positive conditions for the rapid development of the RCFAs. However, the survival of the Associations depends on how effective they are in resisting local government intervention in their business activities. The prevention of government interference should be institutionalised. RCFAs should not be forced to invest funds or act as guarantors for enterprises or individuals applying for loans from banks or the

RCCs. Funds of the Associations should not be expropriated or improperly used by local governments. The Associations should not be given profit targets and directed to hand over their profits to the grass-root-level government authorities. Therefore, establishing a properly functioning democratic and well-monitored system for the RCFAs will prevent local government intervention.

To conclude, in concert with the building of a market-economic system and meeting the need for comprehensive rural development, a better environment must be provided for the development of the RCFAs. Only with this can the Associations become a positive force in promoting agricultural production and rural economic development.

Today, the market-economic system stands as a challenge to the small-scale and backward rural production units and to the isolated rural households. The deficit-stricken government cannot afford to provide subsidies for the agricultural and industrial modernisation process. There exists the ever-worsening trend of funds being invested in non-agricultural production. Under these circumstances, if we put further restrictions on the RCFAs, problems like rural capital outflow and severe shortage of funds for rural economic development will become much worse.

Notes

1 *Chinese Yearbook of Rural Financial Statistics, 1993*, p. 236.
2 *Ibid.*, p. 4.
3 *Zhongguo Nongcun Jinrong (Rural Finance in China)*, No. 2, 1994, p. 64.
4 Wan BaoDuan, 'Several Issues on Ensuring the Healthy Development of the Rural Co-operatives', *Zhongguo Nongcun Jinrong (Rural Finance in China)*, No. 10, 1993, p. 12.
5 *Jinrong Shibao (Financial Times)*, 21 July 1994.

7

CHINA'S FOREIGN EXCHANGE SYSTEM

Gao Xiao Hang and On Kit Tam

This chapter is primarily concerned with the evolution of China's exchange controls and exchange rate system. The system has undergone significant changes to its pre-reform central planning model. Exchange controls and exchange rate policy, together with trade and foreign borrowing policies, are important determinants of China's foreign economic relations. Foreign exchange reform is necessary because the level of the exchange rate represents a key price that links the domestic price system with the international price system. The role of the exchange rate and the way in which it works depends on the extent to which market forces operate. In China the exchange rate also affects the behaviour of domestic and export production enterprises through the foreign exchange retention system and the dual exchange rate regime. At the same time, exchange rate policy is closely related to financial, monetary and fiscal policies.

With the rise of marketisation and openness in the Chinese economy, there is an increasing urgency in the reform of the exchange rate policy.[1] In developing economies undergoing structural changes while maintaining a dual exchange market regime with rising inflation, exchange rate adjustments are often made in response to various forms of monetary and real shocks, usually without the need for the drastic economic reforms that China has attempted. In this chapter an examination of China's experience is undertaken in the context of the country's gradual transition to an open market economy up to the early 1990s.

The chapter is organised as follows: section 1 investigates the changes in China's foreign trade and exchange rate system since reforms began in 1978. Section 2 analyses foreign exchange controls, including quantitative restrictions, the foreign exchange

143

retention system and the dual exchange rate regime. A summary of reforms and events in the foreign trade and exchange system since 1979 is provided in the Appendix. Section 3 examines the real effects of the official exchange rate devaluations during 1978–89 through the measurement of the real effective exchange rate.

1 REFORMS IN THE FOREIGN TRADE AND EXCHANGE SYSTEM SINCE 1979

As an integral part of central planning, the foreign trade and exchange system was isolated from external influences by a number of features in China's economic system before the economic reform:

1 State monopoly over foreign trade. Exports and imports were the responsibility of central government foreign trade corporations; enterprises, local governments and other organisations or individuals were not allowed to carry out foreign trade.

2 Centralised management of foreign exchange. Foreign exchange controls facilitated the requirements of central planning. The value of foreign exchange was fixed. The intention was that external factors, such as changing export demands and international price relativities would not affect the balance of inputs and outputs in production.[2] The inconvertibility of the Chinese currency, combined with the lack of a financial market, was used to prevent external disturbances impacting domestically. In commercial transactions, all foreign exchange earned from foreign trade had to be sold to the state and was sold back to users at a price fixed by the central bank.

3 The volume and composition of exports and imports were determined by the central plan. Enterprises did not have independent financial accounts nor any autonomy in production, sales, input purchasing or pricing. They were not responsible for their profitability. Targets set for enterprises were not based on efficiency or productivity but on physical outputs. Productivity and profitability often had to be sacrificed in order that these targets could be met.

4 Distortion of the domestic price system. The prices of imports and exports were determined by the central plan. Thus, domestic prices are generally not aligned with international prices.

5 The exchange rate of the Chinese currency was deliberately overvalued to support distorted domestic prices and centralised

144

resource allocation. Overvaluation of the currency, however, reduced the competitiveness of domestic production, which competed with imports and undermined the competitiveness of exports. It has been a principal cause of balance of payments difficulties since the 1950s.

6 'Self-sufficiency'. The impact of the exchange rate on domestic prices largely depends on the degree of openness of a country, but China had a very low degree of openness under the self-sufficiency strategy. Between 1968 and 1977, the annual average share of exports and imports in GNP was about 7.4 per cent, while the share of exports was only 3.8 per cent.[3] Therefore, the impact of changes in relative prices would have been negligible even had domestic prices not been distorted. The exchange rate mainly played an accounting role.

China abandoned its 'self-sufficiency' policy in 1978. An outward-oriented development strategy has been adopted with an emphasis on the role of exports in growth. An 'open door' policy has been implemented through increasing foreign trade opportunities and attracting foreign funds. Reform of the foreign trade and exchange system started in 1979 and progressed slowly. More incentives and flexibility were introduced gradually to stimulate export growth and foreign exchange earnings.

Accompanying the 'open door' and export promotion policies is the strategy of coastal area development. In July 1979, the government established four special economic zones (Shenzhen, Zhuhai, Shantou and Xiamen) in Guangdong and Fujian provinces and established special policies and flexible measures for these areas. In 1984, fourteen coastal port cities and Hainan Island were opened to the outside world. Enterprises and provinces in these areas, to varying degrees, enjoy the freedom of directly engaging in foreign trade and international finance.

1979-83

Reform measures were focused on decentralisation of foreign trade, diversification of foreign trade channels and forms, and the integration of production and trade activities within enterprises. The authority to participate in foreign trade was decentralised to local governments, some selected ministries and enterprises to reduce the state monopoly over foreign trade. The chaññels of foreign trade administration and operations were expanded. Special economic zones had some measure of autonomy in foreign trade. Some provinces, municipalities and autonomous regions were also allowed to have their enterprises engage in foreign trade.

Essentially, however, production and export activities were still separated except for those in trade-production corporations. Foreign trade enterprises purchased goods from production enterprises and then exported them. Production enterprises were only responsible for production targets and did not care if their products could be exported or not.

When the authority to engage in foreign trade was delegated downward, authority was merely transferred from one administrative department to a lower one. Enterprises did not become autonomous and were still subject to plan directives. Foreign trade enterprises competed for export goods to fulfil plan targets. Such competition led to an increase in export purchase prices and thus in the unit cost of earning foreign exchange. All the losses and profits were borne by the government though, through the Ministry of Foreign Economic Relations and Trade. Importing inefficiency was similar. These inefficiencies resulted in recentralisation in 1984.

˙1984–6

To avoid competition among domestic enterprises and policy conflicts, management of foreign trade was again concentrated in the Ministry of Foreign Economic Relations and Trade. Guidelines for further reform were proposed, including the setting up of an import-export agency system, separation of the functions of enterprises from those of the government, streamlining and simplifying policy and delegating authority. These guidelines were not, however, followed during 1984–6. The foreign trade system remained heavily centralised with little autonomy for trading or production enterprises;

1987 to the early 1990s

Since 1987, further reforms have been undertaken in the foreign trade system. In March 1987 some foreign trade enterprises were given greater control over their activities. These enterprises had to sign contracts with the state with regard to state export plans, export costs and total export profits and losses. In 1988, the contract responsibility system was expanded to foreign trade on two levels. The first level consisted of contracts between the state and provincial-level local governments as well as state foreign trade corporations. The latter bore responsibility for foreign exchange earnings, the transfer of foreign exchange to the state and for cost-benefit indicators. At the second level, local government and local state foreign trade corporations allocated their contracts with the state to local foreign trade enterprises. Local governments and enterprises were allowed to keep a small part of foreign exchange they earned within the targets of contracts, but a large part of exchange for the overfulfilled targets.

An import-export agency system is being introduced. Instead of purchasing imports and selling exports, foreign trade enterprises will receive commissions, as agents, for services rendered. They will charge handling fees, while productive enterprises will be responsible for profits and losses.

Planning reforms have also been made. Administrative agencies are now separated from foreign trade enterprises. They may not intervene in enterprises' operations. Planning for imports and exports has been reduced to a few goods, hence market influence has been expanded.

An experimental reform aimed at making export enterprises responsible for their own losses and profits was introduced in light industry, including clothing and arts and crafts, in 1988. The reform included abolition of export subsidies and retention of a large share (75 per cent) of foreign exchange earnings.[4] In January 1991, further reforms were introduced. Foreign trade enterprises now have responsibility for their profits and losses.

2 FOREIGN EXCHANGE CONTROLS

The present exchange control system in China, after a round of decentralisation and recentralisation, is still centralised. The State Administration of Exchange Control was established in 1979 to supervise the operations of the Bank of China in all functions connected with the balance of payments. China's foreign exchange control system has a complex multi-level structure. The system is divided into three parts: planning control, administrative control and foreign exchange operational control (Figure 7.1). It applies to both current and capital account transactions. The following analysis primarily focuses on controls relevant to current account transactions.

Quantitative restrictions

Before the import licensing system was employed in 1987, central control and strict restrictions were imposed on importing activity to economise on the use of foreign exchange. Imports required by an enterprise had to be approved by its supervising organisations, then by economic and planning commissions. The commissions reported to local branches of the Ministry of Foreign Economic Relations and Trade and the State Administration of Exchange Control, which then approved or disapproved import proposals according to import plans and regulations. After gaining final approval, enterprises could import through foreign trade companies. This control system, together with the planning system, generated 'rent-seeking' activities. As authority to import was given so rarely and had to be allowed for some enterprises or organisations, it commanded 'economic rent' and enabled these enterprises to make profits.

Under the export purchasing system, decentralised exporting authority, without appropriate price policy and corresponding reform in the fiscal regime, resulted in internal competition among export companies, an increase in the price of export purchase and inefficiency.

Import-export licences and quotas

An import-export licensing system was introduced in 1987 to strengthen controls over importing and exporting activities and to improve the structure of exports and imports. Import or export commodities are divided into three groups. Trade in the first group, comprised of staples and energy-related products, is conducted by appointed foreign trade and trade-production companies of the Ministry of Foreign Economic Relations and Trade or corporations of the ministry and local foreign trade enterprises. The second group, goods whose prices are sensitive in international and domestic markets such as textile exports and most sorts of imports, is assigned to those enterprises which are specialised in the production and trading of these commodities. The first two

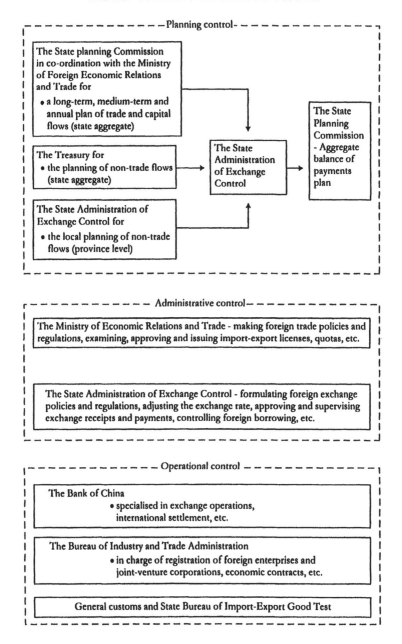

Figure 7.1 The foreign exchange control system in China

groûps are controlled by the Ministry of Foreign Economic Relations and Trade through licence issuing. The third group, mainly insignificant goods, are not controlled by licensing.

In 1988, the number of imported commodities controlled by licensing was increased from forty-five to fifty-three items and the authority to grant import licences for thirty-nine of these items was delegated from the Ministry of Foreign Economic Relations and Trade to province level. The ministry also authorised the appointment of special representatives to work with the ministry and province. In July 1988, the number of export items controlled under licensing was reduced from 257 to 159. Of these, twenty-seven were licensed at the ministry level, forty-one at special representative office level and ninety-one at province level.[5]

In addition to licensing, quotas allocated by the Ministry of Foreign Economic Relations and Trade are also used to control importing and exporting activity.[6] The composition and volume of imports and exports are determined by this system of licences and quotas and the actual value of goods traded does not accurately reflect the outcome which would ensue if business behaviour were profit motivated and a system of price signals prevailed.

Tariffs, import licences and quotas have contributed to a wall of protection in China. The relationship between protection and the level of the exchange rate (e = Chinese yuan per unit of foreign currency) is illustrated in Figure 7.2. The initial demand for and supply of foreign exchange are represented by curves D and S, respectively. The equilibrium exchange rate is e^*. Protection results directly in an increase in the domestic price of imports, hence foreign exchange demand falls from D to D'. At point P, the intersection of curves D' and S, the exchange rate has appreciated to ep. However, this is not an equilibrium rate. Protection also affects the supply side of the foreign exchange market. With higher import prices resulting from protection, the cost of producing exports increases, worsening the country's ability to compete on international markets. The resulting fall in exports induces a reduction in foreign exchange supply which is represented by a shift in the supply curve from S to S'. The equilibrium exchange rate under protection is e.

Under the distorted domestic price system, the Chinese government, however, has maintained the exchange rate at a level similar to ep in order to contain import prices. At ep, the exchange rate is overvalued; the supply of foreign exchange is Q', demand is QP,

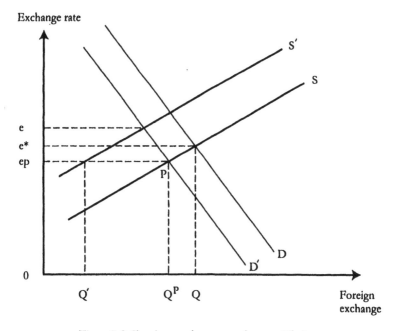

Figure 7.2 Foreign exchange market equilibrium

hence there is an excess demand for foreign exchange. It is often argued that a quota or licence results in a higher domestic price and a lower domestic output than an equivalent tariff.[7] Thus, protection is high when there exist quotas and licences. The exchange rate becomes increasingly overvalued and local producers cannot compete with imports, so there are increased demands for import protection and export subsidies.

Import-export subsidies

Subsidies also influence the consequences of exchange rate changes. Although enterprises have to pay taxes, an import subsidy system has been in operation since 1978, and an export subsidy system to compensate enterprises for losses due to government policy since 1980.

Import subsidies consist of 'price subsidies' and 'policy loss subsidies'. The former refers to subsidies on commodities for which the government has set a domestic sale price much lower

151

than the goods' import cost and is imposed by the government in order to maintain the provision of inputs and staples. 'Price subsidies' are generally used for necessary consumer commodities and materials for agricultural production. Price subsidies for five major imports peaked at 8.8 billion *renminbi* in 1981 and fell to 1.3 billion in 1986.[8] 'Policy loss subsidies' usually refers to subsidies to cover losses which arise from exchange rate changes. For example, a devaluation leads to an increase in import costs. This would cause losses to enterprises which use imported inputs and thus subsidies.

Export subsidies were mainly 'policy loss subsidies'. Between 1980 and 1987 export subsidies increased rapidly (Table 7.1). The two main reasons for the immense export subsidies were incomplete implementation of duty drawback action and exchange rate overvaluation.[9] Before the 1989 devaluation, the official exchange rate was much lower than the country's average cost per unit exchange earnings as shown in Table 7.1. Assuming that the cost of 5 *renminbi* per US dollar earnings is stable after 1986, the devaluation to 4.7221 *renminbi* per US dollar in 1989 is only close to the cost. Although a further devaluation in 1990 (5.1830 *renminbi* per US dollar) implies that foreign exchange costs for most enterprises were covered, an average cost of 6 *renminbi* per US

Table 7.1 Exchange rates, average costs of foreign exchange earnings and export subsidies, 1979–90

Years	Exchange rate (renmimbi/$)	Export cost (renminbi/$)	Export subsidies (billion renminbi)
1979	1.5550	2.53	—
1980	1.4984	2.50	3.479
1981	1.7045	2.61	1.118
1982	1.8925	2.86	6.135
1983	1.9757	3.22	11.394
1984	2.3200	—	6.937
1985	2.9367	4.00	2.802
1986	3.4528	5.00	8.000
1987	3.7221	—	—
1988	3.7221	—	—
1989	4.7221	—	—
1990	5.1830	5.13	—

Sources: Chan (1989); *China Trade Report*, August 1987: 3, 1991: 16; State Bureau of Statistics: *Statistical Yearbook of China, 1990*, Beijing, 1991; State Bureau of Statistics, 1986, *Data on Finance*: 261 (mimeo); Chen and Yang (1990).

dollar in special economic zones, compared with the exchange rate, still leads to a possible loss in these localities.

In addition to the above direct subsidies, a variety of indirect or disguised subsidies have been widely adopted for both imports and exports. First, the Fund for Development of Major Export and Domestic Enterprises (*zhongdian chukou qiye fazhan jijing* and *zhongdian qiye fazhan jijing*) was set up to provide these enterprises with access to funds for technological upgrading. The definition of *major* enterprises, however, varies from industry to industry, ministry to ministry, province to province and even city to city with the consequence that the government subsidises a wide range of enterprises.

The same situation also arose with bank loans. The Bank of China, other specialised banks and the local banking system granted export enterprises and technically advanced enterprises priority in obtaining loans so that they could meet their short-term demands for operating capital and foreign exchange. After 1978, when the government wanted to attract private direct foreign investment, it attempted to do so through the use of fiscal incentives and by allowing foreign firms to borrow in China from government banks at subsidised interest rates. In addition, enterprises obtained other subsidies through the dual exchange rate regime and foreign exchange retention system. These will be discussed in the following section.

The various subsidies are costly to the economy, and impact particularly on the budget. In 1988, subsidies for foreign trade reached 22.4 billion *renminbi* or 11 per cent of budget revenue.[10] Subsidies also require an enormous amount of administrative support which is costly, both directly and indirectly, and has unanticipated side-effects. In fact, enterprises' losses come in part from inefficient operation and in part from price and exchange rate policies such as the overvalued exchange rate. However, the two sources of loss are hard to distinguish in practice, and government subsidies also contribute to enterprise inefficiency. As the enterprise contract responsibility system was implemented comprehensively in export enterprises and other policy incentives were introduced to exports, such as duty drawback action, continual devaluations, settlement of exchange markets and improvement of the exchange retention system, export subsidies were removed from the light manufacturing, clothing and arts-and-crafts sectors in 1988 and from the remainder of exports in 1991. Import subsidies are still in force and increase with currency devaluations. Abolition of import subsidies requires further import liberalisation and a reduction of tariff and non-tariff barriers.

The foreign exchange retention system

In 1978, a retention system for exchange allocation was introduced at the provincial level with the aim of providing funds for local development. Each provincial authority and its exchange-earning enterprises were entitled to retain a certain proportion of foreign exchange conditional on over-fulfilment of export quotas assigned to them under the central plans. Local governments and enterprises were not actually given foreign exchange but were granted entitlement quotas which could be swapped at prices (swap rate) usually higher than the official exchange rate. After formal foreign exchange markets (swap centres) were established in most provinces and cities in 1988, instead of the imposed price, the swap rate has been floating and determined by supply and demand in these markets, although some controls still apply. Thus, by selling their quotas at the swap rate, enterprises can obtain higher *renminbi* revenue, and hence the system is an incentive for enterprises to expand exports. Since export enterprises generally suffer from high export costs and losses, the revenue from the discrepancy between the swap rate and the official rate is in fact a sort of export subsidy. The utilisation of the quotas initially had to be approved by the central government. After 1988 direct controls on the utilisation of retained foreign exchange were replaced by a 'guidance list' which encourages imports of raw materials and equipment for agriculture and staple goods.[11]

Since 1982, the retention system has been based on actual performance (foreign exchange earnings) rather than on procurement performance (the fulfilment of export plans)[12] and extended to non-trade exchange earnings, such as income from tourism. The retention rate plays an important role in foreign exchange control and allocation. The retention rate is the proportion of total foreign exchange earnings retained by enterprises or local governments. Through the retention rate system, foreign exchange is distributed between central government and local governments and enterprises.

In 1984, special economic zones and their enterprises enjoyed a 100 per cent retention rate; autonomous regions 50 per cent;

Guandong and Fujian provinces, which had special policy status, 30 per cent; and other provinces 25 per cent. The remaining foreign exchange earnings were allocated to the central government.[13] Subsequently, the rate for local governments and enterprises (excluding special economic zones) was increased to 40 per cent in 1985.[14] As such the retention system operated as a sort of subsidy for priority regions and is therefore a regionally based retention system.

The regionally based retention system tended to encourage competition among the local authorities as it provided subsidies for some local groups. Under this system the interests of enterprises in non-priority areas were ignored and sacrificed. Higher retention rates in special economic zones and coastal port cities enabled the foreign trade enterprises in these areas to earn higher *renminbi* income. These enterprises therefore rushed to the low retention rate areas to purchase exportable goods which they then exported to foreigners. Competition among these domestic buyers contributed consequently to increased purchase prices and export costs. The country's average cost of earning one US dollar from exports increased from 3.22 *renminbi* in 1983 to 5.00 *renminbi* in 1986 (Table 7.1). Increasing export costs rendered enterprises less competitive. Non-priority enterprises suffered even greater losses, generating a greater need for subsidies. The result was a loss of national efficiency.

In 1987 the policy focus switched to encouraging the growth of non-traditional and labour-intensive exports and hence improving the export product mix. As more attention was paid to products and sectors, an average retention rate of 4 per cent was added to the rate for enterprises in the coastal port areas which produced light manufacturing goods for export. For machinery and electronic export goods, a 30 per cent retention rate was introduced and an additional 5 per cent was allocated to the local government department in charge of these enterprises (raising their share from 5 to 10 per cent). The state's share remained constant at 50 per cent and the share allocated to foreign trade companies was reduced from 15 to 10 per cent.[15] Moreover, three sectors – clothing, light industry and arts-and-crafts – were an experiment involving increased retention rates of 75 per cent.

In January 1988, the local retention system was redefined as follows: the rate applied to special economic zones was reduced to 80 per cent; the rate for the three selected industries was increased from 75 per cent to 80 per cent in all areas; and a rate of 100 per cent was introduced for all electronic equipment and machinery producers.[16] After the implementation of the contract responsibility system in export enterprises, the local retention system was maintained for foreign exchange earned in the course of contract fulfilment, with different retention rates for different areas. Exchange earned on production in excess of contract volumes attracted a uniform retention rate, that is, the same rate was applied everywhere in order that a more equal environment for competitors could be fostered and special economic zones' privileges were curbed. Generally, local governments and enterprises retained 25 per cent of foreign exchange and 30–40 per cent of non-trade foreign exchange, but poor mountainous areas and enterprises engaging in new trade ventures or encouraged products (such as machinery and electronic products) were allowed a 100 per cent rate.[17]

Following the scrapping of export subsidies from 1 January 1991 and the comprehensive implementation of loss-profit responsibility (*Zifu Yingkui*), the retention system and rates have been further changed. The features of the new system are: (1) the retention rate varies according to contract fulfilment, with a smaller share (usually 40 per cent) allocated to enterprises for foreign exchange earnings required by contracts and a larger share (usually 70 per cent) for earnings stemming from over-fulfilment of contracts; (2) different retention rates are applied to different types of export product with the aim of encouraging non-traditional exports such as machinery and electronic products and discouraging the export of primary products such as petroleum; (3) introduction of surrender charges, that is, the central government will pay enterprises 30 per cent of foreign exchange earnings surrendered by the enterprises at the country's average swap rate instead of the official rate to compensation for enterprises' losses.[18] These principles apply to all localities. The new system is aimed at slowing the growing independence of regional governments and promoting non-traditional exports.

However, the arrangement still involves foreign exchange entitlement quotas, not the actual supply of hard foreign currency. Both quotas and retention rates are determined and allocated by the government. With the foreign exchange generated by enterprises, the government builds up state foreign reserves, and at the same time it allocates entitlement quotas and the right to utilise earnings from foreign trade enterprises. Thus, the possibility arises of multiple claims for the same amount of foreign exchange because of discrepancies and time lags in the granting of the entitlement by the central government and their actual use by enterprises and local authorities. This situation could result in an unintended expansion in the use of foreign currency, which might have to be accommodated by increased overseas borrowing, depletion of reserves and cut-backs in present and future expenditures, all of which would inevitably throw the original planned balances into chaos, as happened in 1984/85.[19] Further reforms were introduced into the foreign trade and exchange system in 1988 and 1991 which involved comprehensive implementation of the contract responsibility system (including loss-and-profit responsibility), abolition of export subsidies and reform measures in the retention system. However, the foundations of the multiple claims – the entitlement quota system – have been maintained.

It is now commonly accepted that further reform in this area should aim to change the system of exchange entitlement to one involving immediate conversion of *renminbi* into foreign currencies, so that the existing dual control mechanism and associated problems of multiple use are eliminated. Furthermore, the corresponding development and rationalisation of markets for foreign exchange is necessary for a solution of the above problem.

Foreign exchange markets and the dual exchange rate regime

One striking feature of the Chinese economy since 1978 has been the co-existence of plan and market prices in many areas of the economy. Within the foreign exchange system, foreign exchange plans and foreign exchange markets co-exist to manage foreign exchange; the central plan and retention system co-determine the distribution of foreign exchange; and both official rates and swap rates apply to the foreign exchange rate regime. The duality in the exchange system is in essence a reflection of the dual price system and the direct result of the dual foreign exchange distribution system discussed previously.

Prior to 1979, enterprises were not allowed to hold hard currency or import at will under the centrally planned system. Thus, there was no supply of and demand for foreign exchange among enterprises. With the development of the foreign exchange retention system since 1979, retained foreign exchange has provided the basis for an exchange market. Retained foreign exchange is distributed to a large number of enterprises and units although each unit only holds a very limited amount.[20] This tends to influence the efficiency of foreign exchange utilisation and has meant that foreign exchange markets have developed gradually.

A formal dual exchange rate system was introduced in January 1981 to adjust the overvalued exchange rate but without the domestic sector and non-commodity trade being influenced by exchange rate changes: the government set an internal exchange rate (2.8 *renminbi* per US dollar) for commodity trade and maintained the official rate (1.53 *renminbi* per dollar) for non-commodity trade. As the US dollar depreciated in 1984, however, the official exchange rate was devalued to 2.79 *renminbi* per US dollar, and the gap between the official and internal rates gradually disappeared. Thus, from January 1985, the internal exchange rate was abolished and the official exchange rate system returned to a unified regime. In fact, however, another kind of exchange rate existed at this same time: the swap rate.

In October 1980, the opportunity for Chinese enterprises to swap foreign exchange was introduced by the Trust and Consultancy Company of the Bank of China for state enterprises which had no access to the state foreign exchange allocation quota.[21] Chinese enterprises and units were allowed to swap (sell and buy, or lend and borrow) their foreign exchange quotas and/or foreign currencies at a state-determined rate at the Bank of China in twelve selected cites (Beijing, Shanghai, Tianjing, Guangzhou, Qingdao, Dalian, Fuzhou, Nanning, Nanjing, Hangzhou, Wuhan, Shijiazhuang).[22] These were the precursors of subsequent swap centres but at that time swap activities were limited to state enterprises or units, with no swap facility available for foreign enterprises. The share of retained foreign exchange in total exchange was rather small and its price was determined by the government which allowed a 10 per cent margin up or down on the internal exchange rate (2.80 *re–minbi* per US dollar), that is, the highest possible swap rate was 3.08 *renminbi* per dollar.

In October 1985, Shanghai increased the swap rate to 4.00 *renminbi* per dollar in an experimental reform.[23] In December 1985, with approval of the State Council and the People's Bank of China, Shenzhen swap centre was established. Subsequently, other swap centres were set up in Zhuhai, Xiamen and Shantou special economic zones.[24] In early 1986 transactions were extended to swap activities between foreign investment enterprises.[25] There were then two main forms of trading, one for domestic Chinese enterprises (officially called exchange adjustment centres) and the other for foreign enterprises (called foreign exchange trading centres). The two channels were segmented and foreign enterprises were not allowed to participate in the swap activities. Meanwhile, the allowable swap rate was raised to a 1-*renminbi* margin up or down on an official rate of 3.20 *renminbi* per US dollar, implying a maximum rate of 4.20 *renminbi* per US dollar[26] for the country as a whole, while for special economic zones, Hainan and foreign enterprises, the swap rate was allowed to float. Its level was determined by the situation of demand and supply. In late 1986, control of swap business was transferred from the Bank of China to the People's Bank of China.

Although two kinds of exchange rate existed during 1980-7, a market for retained foreign exchange had not been established country-wide. The swap rate at that time was still a kind of official rate and was determined by the government on the basis of the official rate and the unit costs of foreign exchange earnings. Participants were limited to their own locality's state enterprises and units. Furthermore, the process of swap activities was invariably handled directly by the local Administration of Exchange Control, which in effect co-ordinated and re-allocated the available surplus foreign exchange quota to the requesting units.[27] The acquired quota under the adjustment arrangement could only be used for specifically approved expenditures. Moreover, enterprises were not able to purchase foreign currencies with a quota if they did not also have an approved target for foreign exchange spending. There was, however, an even more important constraint on the effective mobilisation of foreign funds under this adjustment process. This involved the restrictions enforced by the local authorities to prevent any outflow of their exchange quota from their jurisdiction.[28] Thus, the whole adjustment process merely amounted to an internal re-allocation of foreign exchange within each local economy. Although there is no available data on the actual amount of currencies that changed hands in this way, there are indications that the volume was not at all significant, with a large number of willing buyers and few sellers.[29]

Since 1988, with the implementation of the contract responsibility system, the decentralisation of foreign trade authority and the redefinition of the foreign exchange retention system, swap centres emerged in most parts of China.[30] By February 1989, there were thirty-nine local swap centres in provinces, municipalities, autonomous regions, special economic zones and the singly-planned cities; and the national swap centre in Beijing. In 1988, the total value of currency swapped through swap centres was 6.264 billion dollars, accounting for one third in national retained foreign exchanges and 18 per cent in national imports.[31] At these centres the exchange rate is set through a managed floating system and determined by market forces instead of directly by the government. Swap activity between foreign enterprises has been extended to exchange between foreign and domestic enterprises. Local governments have been allowed to swap their retained foreign exchange. Some cities (Shanghai, Shenzhen, Xiamen, Ningbo and Quanzhou) have opened swap businesses to individuals[32] and controls over foreign exchange use for specially approved expenditure categories have been removed. However, the restrictions on exchange flows between local markets discussed above are still a problem.[33]

Figure 7.3 presents the dual exchange system and foreign exchange flow. Among the three broad sources of foreign exchange, remittances enter via the secondary market, while aid and foreign borrowing enter via the official system. Through the foreign exchange retention system, export earnings are divided into two parts: one is official or central foreign exchange which is owned and allocated by the central government; the other is retained foreign exchange owned by local governments and enterprises. Therefore, local governments and enterprises have two sources of foreign exchange: retained exchange and centrally allocated exchange. The allocation and utilisation of central exchange are still subject to the plan mechanism, and its price exchange is mainly subject to the market mechanism and can be traded on the secondary market at managed floating prices. Sellers (exporters) sell their retained foreign exchange and get *renminbi* revenue in return for exporting. Buyers (importers) purchase foreign currency by selling *renminbi*. Import activities and other foreign exchange are subject to import licences and quantitative controls. After the 1991 reform, with the abolition of export subsidies and an increase in retention rate, retained exchange and the exchange market have been playing a more important role in influencing enterprise behaviour.

Under the dual exchange rate regime, the two markets do not

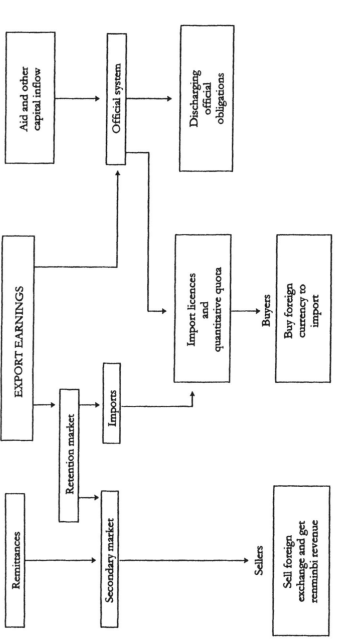

Figure 7.3 The dual exchange system and foreign exchange flow in China

move together. Table 7.2 presents exchange rate changes in both markets between 1981 and 1990. Between August 1986 and November 1989 when the official rate was fixed, the parallel rate exhibited a tendency to depreciate. This put pressure on the official rate to devalue. In December 1989 the official rate was devalued by 21.2 per cent. Subsequently the parallel rate appreciated about 3 per cent in 1990.

One feature of China's dual exchange rate regime is that as a substitute for direct export subsidies and an export promotion measure, the main purpose of the secondary market is to provide a channel for export enterprises to compensate their losses. Due to domestic price inflation in recent years, increasing costs of export production have resulted in widespread losses in export enterprises and have discouraged export growth. In this environment, the foreign exchange market was opened and enterprises can now exchange their entitlement quotas for *renminbi* at near-market

Table 7.2 Renminbi exchange rate devaluations, 1981–90 (*renminbi/$*)

	Official rate	Parallel rate (internal/swap)
1/ 1/1981		2.8000
3/ 1/1985	2.7900	3.0800
30/10/1985	3.2000	4.2000
15/ 7/1986	3.7200	
16/12/1989	4.7221	.
17/11/1990	5.1830	
1988		5.8036[a]
1989		5.9075[b]
1990		5.7500[c]

Sources: M. Xie, and Y. Luo, (1989) *Forty Years of the Chinese Economic Development*, (Beijing: Renmin Chubanshe, 134); B. Chen, (1989). 'Probe into the *Renminbi* Exchange Rate Reform', *International Finance Study,* October: 17; C. Xiao, (1989) 'Should and How *Renminbi* Exchange Rate Against the US Dollar be Adjusted', *International Finance Study,* November: 15; State Bureau of Statistics: *Statistical Yearbook of China, 1990*: 864, Beijing, 1991.

Notes: (a) Annual average rate, calculated from five cities' (Shanghai, Tianjing, Guangzhou, Dalian and Qingdao) weighted average rates (*Almanac of China's Finance and Banking,* 1989: 148).
(b) Year-end rate, calculated from four cities' (Shanghai, Nanjing, Xiamen, Dalian) year-end rates (*Chinese Economic News,* No. 3, 15/1/1990).
(c) Spot rate on 30 September 1990, calculated from four cities' (Guangzhou, Nanjing, Shanghai and Hainan) spot rates (*Chinese Economic News,* No. 40, 15/10/1990).

prices (swap rate), which are usually higher than the official rate, so they can get higher *renminbi* revenue in compensation for their export losses. The revenue from foreign exchange swaps has now become one of the main sources of compensation for export losses (others are government subsidies and tariff-drawback action). For machinery and electronic enterprises, 35 per cent of export compensation is reported to come from the trade of foreign exchange at swap centres.[34]

Following the abolition of government subsidies and an increase of the retention rate for enterprises in January 1991, the foreign exchange market and swap activities are playing an even more important role in replacing direct subsidies and compensating for export losses. Government intervention is maintained in the secondary market to help enterprises achieve indirect subsidies. A floor price and ceiling price are used. With the existence of indirect subsidies and intervention, however, the effect of exchange rate changes on export production is distorted.

The above discussion indicates that exchange controls have been in force in the Chinese economy since the 1978 reforms, although their key features are quite different from those which generally apply in centrally planned and free market economies. Aside from tariffs and duties, subsidies and quantitative restrictions, the dual exchange rate regime together with the foreign exchange retention system is also a sort of exchange control. These controls can affect the consequences of exchange rate changes.

3 MEASURING THE REAL EFFECTIVE EXCHANGE RATE

After a long period of rigid exchange rate policy and overvaluation, official exchange rate devaluations have been used since 1978 in China to stimulate exports and restrict imports. However, given the much stronger inflationary pressure during the reform period, changes in the nominal exchange rate do not reflect shifts in price competitiveness. To address this question, it is necessary to investigate movements in the real effective exchange rate.

The real exchange rate is a key price in the economic system and changes in the real exchange rate affect the allocation of resources, the structure and level of production, foreign trade flows and the balance of payments.[35] It is the real exchange rate, not the nominal rate, that affects economic behaviour. The nominal exchange rate is used as a policy instrument in China and hence is treated as an exogenous variable in a model of the economic system, but the real exchange rate is an endogenous variable that responds to policy-induced shocks, i.e. changes in exogenous variables. There is a causal connection between nominal and real exchange rates in any situation. Changes in other exogenous macroeconomic variables influence the real effect of the nominal exchange rate and hence cause the deviation of the nominal exchange rate from its real rate. Devaluation leads to a new set of fixed nominal and effective exchange rates, but domestic inflation in excess of the world rate might result in a return to the former real situation. Export subsidies or duties and trade protection also reinforce or offset the real effect of the nominal exchange rate. International competitiveness is reduced if domestic inflation is higher than the weighted average inflation of trading partners. The nominal exchange rate would be devalued more than the real exchange rate.

Bilateral real effective exchange rate

The measurement of the real exchange rate was traditionally based on the notion of purchasing power parity. According to that approach, the real exchange rate was defined at the nominal rate multiplied by the ratio of the foreign to the domestic price indices. The real exchange rate has recently been defined as the domestic relative price of tradable to non-tradable goods.[36]

In this definition, the balance of the trade account depends on the relative price of tradable to non-tradable goods and not on the purchasing power parity definition of the real exchange rate. This definition captures the degree of competitiveness of the tradable-goods sector in the home country by defining the current account as the excess supply of tradable goods; it assumes that the supply of tradable goods depends positively on the relative price of those goods while demand depends negatively on this relative price and positively on real income. It thus signals changes in the economy's competitiveness. With other things given, a higher real exchange rate indicates a higher degree of competitiveness of the tradables sector.

Adopting Edwards' definition,[37] a bilateral exchange rate between the domestic currency and a foreign currency can be defined as follows. Assuming no taxes on trade, let

E = nominal exchange rate (amount of domestic currency per unit of foreign currency)

PT^* = world price of tradable goods in terms of foreign currency

PN = price of nontradable goods

e = the real exchange rate

The real exchange rate can be defined as

$$e = E \cdot \frac{PT^*}{PN} \tag{1}$$

In the context of the tradable–non-tradable relative price definition, a major practical problem is that tradable and non-tradable goods data are for the most part not available. Some alternatives such as the consumer price index (domestic and foreign), the wholesale price index, the gross domestic product deflator and the wage rate index have thus been suggested as proxies for the construction of a real exchange rate index. Edwards (1989) suggested that a more practical approach would be to construct the real exchange rate using components of the traditional price indices. Two methods of real exchange rate estimation are used here.

The first method follows Edwards (1989) and uses the foreign wholesale price index in the numerator and the domestic consumer price index in the denominator. There are several advantages to this approach. It has been argued that the consumer price index contains a broader range of goods and services, both tradables and non-tradables, while the wholesale price index mainly contains tradables.[38] For example, in *International Financial Statistics* the consumer price index is defined as an indicator reflecting 'changes in the cost of acquiring a fixed basket of goods and services by the average consumer'. While the wholesale price index 'covers a mixture of prices of agricultural and industrial goods at various stages of production and distribution, inclusive of imports and import duties'.[39] By using the wholesale price index for foreign countries (trading partners) and the consumer price index for the home country, emphasis is put on changes in the relative price of tradables to non-tradables and foreign to domestic prices rather than on changes within tradables or non-tradables. The combination of the consumer and wholesale price indices also helps overcome the shortcomings of the two indices. By using components of the wholesale price index in the numerator, this approach provides an appropriate measure of changes in the tradable goods sectors in the trading partners. By using components of the consumer price index in the denominator, this method provides a comprehensive measure of changes in competitiveness for the home country and minimises the bias against the tradable goods sectors. The cost involved in building these series is relatively low and cross-country comparisons can easily be made.

The second method uses foreign wholesale price indices in the numerator and the domestic index of agricultural goods in the denominator. China's wholesale price index is not available. The reason behind the use of the agricultural price index is that it reflects price adjustments and contains higher inflation than the consumer price index. For comparison purposes with use of the consumer price index, therefore, use of the agricultural price index for China is necessary.

The above discussion refers only to bilateral relationships between currencies and not to multilateral relationships. As Edwards points out, 'in a world where the main currencies are floating, there are many different bilateral rates.'[40]

Multilateral or trade-weighted real effective exchange rates

A real trade-weighted exchange rate should take into account the multilateral behaviour of trading partners' exchange rates. China's exchange rate is pegged to a basket of eighteen major trading partners' exchange rates. The choice of the eighteen foreign currencies to which the *renminbi* is pegged depends on the importance of these countries in their trade with China. For this reason, equation (1) becomes:

$$\text{REER}jt = \frac{\sum_{l=1}^{k} Ait Eit Pit^*}{Pjt} \tag{2}$$

where

$\text{REER}jt$ = index of the real effective trade-weighted exchange rate in period t for the home country j

Ait = the trade weight corresponding to partner i in period t

Eit = index of the nominal rate between countries i and j in period t, $i = 1, \ldots, k$ represents k partner countries

Pit^* = (wholesale) price index of the ith partner in period t

Pjt = (consumer) price index of the home country in period t

Table 7.3 Export weights of China's eighteen major trading partners, 1978–89 (per cent)

Country	1978	1979	1980	1981	1982	1983	1984	1985	1986	1987	1988	1989
Total	1.000	1.000	1.000	1.000	1.000	1.000	1.000	1.000	1.000	1.000	1.000	1.000
Australia	0.018	0.016	0.017	0.016	0.015	0.011	0.012	0.009	0.009	0.011	0.010	0.010
Austria	0.001	0.001	0.001	0.001	0.001	0.001	0.001	0.001	0.001	0.001	0.001	0.001
Belgium	0.007	0.007	0.007	0.007	0.009	0.009	0.007	0.008	0.009	0.008	0.006	0.006
Canada	0.007	0.016	0.011	0.011	0.012	0.013	0.014	0.012	0.013	0.013	0.010	0.010
Denmark	0.003	0.003	0.003	0.003	0.003	0.003	0.003	0.004	0.004	0.004	0.003	0.002
Finland	0.001	0.001	0.001	0.001	0.001	0.001	0.001	0.001	0.001	0.002	0.003	0.001
France	0.027	0.024	0.026	0.018	0.019	0.014	0.012	0.012	0.013	0.015	0.014	0.012
Germany	0.049	0.048	0.054	0.055	0.051	0.055	0.043	0.037	0.043	0.042	0.040	0.039
Hong Kong	0.406	0.370	0.349	0.346	0.344	0.371	0.364	0.349	0.423	0.468	0.495	0.518
Italy	0.025	0.031	0.026	0.017	0.016	0.016	0.017	0.015	0.016	0.019	0.020	0.017
Japan	0.261	0.288	0.306	0.312	0.320	0.289	0.285	0.296	0.206	0.217	0.215	0.198
Netherlands	0.030	0.028	0.028	0.030	0.019	0.021	0.018	0.016	0.020	0.020	0.021	0.017
Norway	0.001	0.001	0.001	0.001	0.001	0.001	0.001	0.001	0.001	0.004	0.002	0.001
Singapore	0.037	0.031	0.032	0.044	0.042	0.037	0.068	0.101	0.052	0.046	0.040	0.040
Sweden	0.004	0.004	0.004	0.004	0.004	0.003	0.003	0.003	0.003	0.003	0.004	0.004
Switzerland	0.016	0.017	0.015	0.008	0.007	0.006	0.006	0.007	0.008	0.007	0.005	0.004
UK	0.056	0.050	0.043	0.027	0.020	0.038	0.018	0.017	0.062	0.017	0.018	0.015
US	0.042	0.063	0.075	0.099	0.116	0.111	0.128	0.114	0.114	0.103	0.092	0.104

Source: State Bureau of Statistics, Statistical Yearbook of China, Beijing, 1981–90

Equation (2) is used to estimate China's real export- and import-weighted exchange rates. If the consumer price rises faster in China than the weighted average wholesale price index of its trading partners, the value of the real trade-weighted exchange rate will be less than that of the nominal exchange rate, implying real appreciation and vice versa.

Data

The data for estimation include export weights, import weights, price indices and nominal exchange rates.

(1) Export weights. Hong Kong and Japan are the two leading destinations for China's exports. Exports to these countries comprised 65 per cent of total exports to the eighteen countries whose exchange rates were used in the exchange rate basket for the period 1981–7. Over this period Japan's weight decreased and Hong Kong's weight increased. The combined share of total exports accounted for by Hong Kong and Japan plus China's other three major trading partners – the United States, Germany and Singapore – is more than 85 per cent. Exchange rate and relative price changes in these five countries have a major influence on changes in China's real export exchange rate. The export weights of China's eighteen major trading partners are given in Table 7.3.

(2) Import weights. The import weights of the eighteen countries or regions are presented in Table 7.4. Japan is the largest source of China's imports. In the early 1980s the United States was the second largest source of imports, but imports from the United States have been falling. Hong Kong has replaced the United States as the second largest source of imports.

(3) Price indices. The consumer and agricultual price indices of China and its eighteen trading partners' wholesale price indices are given in Table 7.5. These indices, averaged according to export or import weights, are taken as proxies for price changes in these economies relative to China.

As reported in official sources, the Chinese agricultural price index always rises faster than the consumer price index and thus measures a higher rate of inflation. These price indices might be much lower than their true values.[41] In spite of this potential under-valuation, over time the official indices still reflect certain trends. The price index data in this study come from the IMF's *International Finance Statistics* (1978–90). Both consumer and agricultural price

Table 7.4 Import weights of China's eighteen major trading partners, 1978–89 (per cent)

Country	1978	1979	1980	1981	1982	1983	1984	1985	1986	1987	1988	1989
Total	1.000	1.000	1.000	1.000	1.000	1.000	1.000	1.000	1.000	1.000	1.000	1.000
Australia	0.095	0.091	0.071	0.043	0.064	0.038	0.044	0.034	0.041	0.038	0.026	0.034
Austria	0.003	0.003	0.003	0.003	0.004	0.004	0.006	0.005	0.009	0.007	0.005	0.005
Belgium	0.009	0.008	0.008	0.008	0.012	0.015	0.010	0.007	0.010	0.007	0.009	0.008
Canada	0.076	0.056	0.056	0.068	0.088	0.099	0.052	0.034	0.030	0.040	0.044	0.024
Denmark	0.003	0.003	0.003	0.003	0.003	0.009	0.004	0.004	0.004	0.005	0.004	0.003
Finland	0.004	0.004	0.004	0.005	0.003	0.004	0.005	0.004	0.004	0.005	0.004	0.003
France	0.033	0.036	0.021	0.023	0.016	0.040	0.018	0.021	0.021	0.026	0.023	0.032
Germany	0.137	0.160	0.090	0.078	0.068	0.076	0.062	0.071	0.104	0.089	0.080	0.053
Hong Kong	0.010	0.019	0.038	0.073	0.092	0.106	0.137	0.142	0.164	0.242	0.280	0.286
Italy	0.026	0.028	0.017	0.020	0.023	0.019	0.022	0.027	0.034	0.036	0.036	0.042
Japan	0.410	0.350	0.349	0.361	0.274	0.344	0.393	0.444	0.362	0.289	0.258	0.240
Netherlands	0.007	0.007	0.007	0.006	0.007	0.007	0.008	0.007	0.009	0.006	0.009	0.011
Norway	0.001	0.001	0.001	0.001	0.003	0.003	0.004	0.004	0.002	0.002	0.004	0.004
Singapore	0.006	0.010	0.013	0.006	0.007	0.007	0.008	0.007	0.016	0.017	0.023	0.034
Sweden	0.007	0.007	0.007	0.006	0.005	0.009	0.008	0.007	0.009	0.009	0.006	0.007
Switzerland	0.039	0.018	0.016	0.010	0.012	0.015	0.009	0.007	0.015	0.015	0.012	0.012
UK	0.039	0.044	0.037	0.014	0.019	0.034	0.024	0.022	0.030	0.026	0.021	0.024
US	0.095	0.164	0.259	0.272	0.302	0.172	0.187	0.150	0.137	0.140	0.155	0.179

Source: State Bureau of Statistics, Statistical Yearbook of China, Beijing, 1981–90

Table 7.5 Price indices of China and its eighteen major trading partners, 1978–89 (per cent, 1978 = 100)

Country	1978	1979	1980	1981	1982	1983	1984	1985	1986	1987	1988	1989
Australia	100.0	122.1	130.9	142.0	154.6	167.1	176.3	187.8	198.3	212.8	228.8	244.0
Austria	100.0	99.2	113.1	122.2	126.1	126.9	131.7	135.1	127.9	125.5	125.1	127.4
Belgium	100.0	103.6	112.5	121.7	131.0	137.9	148.1	148.1	138.5	135.1	133.8	142.6
Canada	100.0	122.7	129.9	143.0	151.7	156.9	163.2	167.7	169.1	173.5	180.4	185.2
China [a]	100.0	102.0	109.5	112.3	114.6	116.9	120.0	133.8	141.8	152.3	186.3	216.7
China [b]	100.0	122.1	130.9	138.6	141.6	147.9	153.8	167.0	177.8	199.0	220.5	—
China [c]	100.0	104.9	123.8	130.7	136.4	142.2	150.1	184.6	204.6	230.6	315.6	391.6
China [d]	100.0	155.3	177.2	196.5	201.1	219.8	234.5	267.5	294.4	347.4	401.2	—
Denmark	100.0	110.1	128.2	148.7	164.1	171.8	184.6	191.0	178.2	176.9	185.5	195.0
Finland	100.0	112.5	127.7	144.1	154.4	163.0	171.8	179.4	170.1	171.6	178.6	187.6
France [e]	100.0	113.3	123.3	125.0	152.0	168.8	191.2	198.9	203.9	210.7	216.3	223.9
Germany	100.0	104.8	112.7	121.5	128.7	130.6	134.4	137.7	134.2	130.8	132.5	136.6
Hong Kong [f]	100.0	111.5	128.4	150.2	166.9	183.5	198.9	205.1	211.1	239.4	239.0	263.3
Italy	100.0	115.5	138.7	162.8	185.4	203.5	224.5	241.1	239.0	245.2	256.6	273.0
Japan	100.0	107.3	126.4	128.2	130.5	127.6	127.3	125.8	114.3	110.0	108.9	111.7
Netherlands	100.0	102.8	111.1	119.2	125.9	127.6	133.2	135.3	131.4	130.3	127.9	132.3
Norway	100.0	108.8	125.0	138.8	147.5	156.3	166.3	175.0	178.8	190.0	199.7	210.1
Singapore	100.0	114.4	136.8	142.1	136.1	131.2	130.4	127.4	108.2	116.3	114.1	117.1
Sweden	100.0	112.8	142.3	160.3	178.2	139.0	150.0	158.0	154.0	158.0	166.7	179.4
Switzerland	100.0	103.8	109.2	115.5	118.4	119.0	122.9	125.7	120.7	118.3	120.9	126.1
UK	100.0	110.9	126.4	138.6	149.2	157.3	167.0	176.2	184.2	191.3	200.0	210.2
US	100.0	112.5	128.4	140.1	142.9	144.7	148.1	147.5	143.1	147.0	152.7	160.2

Sources: United Nations, Statistical Indicators for Asia and the Pacific, New York, 1979–88; Asian Development Bank, Key Indicators of Developing Asian and Pacific Countries, Manila, 1990; 'Prices and Trends: Economic Indicators, Selected Asian Countries', Far Eastern Economic Review, 11 July 1991; The IMF, International Financial Statistics Yearbook, Washington, 1979–91.

Note: [a] Consumer price index figures. [b] Agricultural price index figures. [c] Revised consumer price index figures. [d] Revised agricultural price index figures. [e] Consumer price index figures just for 1986 and 1987. [f] Consumer price index figures.

Table 7.6 Nominal exchange rates for China and its eighteen major trading partners, 1978–89 (currency units/US$)

Country	1978	1979	1980	1981	1982	1983
Australia	0.8700	0.8900	0.8800	0.8700	0.9830	1.1080
Austria	14.5220	13.3680	12.9380	15.9270	17.0590	17.9630
Belgium	31.4920	29.3190	29.2420	37.1290	45.6910	51.1320
Canada	1.1407	1.1714	1.1692	1.1989	1.2337	1.2324
China	1.6836	1.5550	1.4984	1.7045	1.8925	1.9757
Denmark	5.5150	5.2610	5.6360	7.1230	8.3320	9.1450
Finland	4.1173	3.8953	3.7301	4.3153	4.8204	5.5701
France	4.5131	4.2544	4.2256	5.4346	6.5721	7.6213
Germany	2.0086	1.8329	1.8177	2.2600	2.4266	2.5533
Hong Kong[a]	4.6930	5.0030	4.9760	5.5670	6.0700	7.2650
Italy	848.7000	830.9000	856.4000	1136.8000	1352.5000	1518.8000
Japan	210.4400	219.1400	226.7400	220.5400	249.0800	237.5100
Netherlands	2.1636	2.006	1.9881	2.4952	2.6702	2.8541
Norway	5.2423	5.0641	4.9392	5.7395	6.4540	7.2964
Singapore	2.2740	2.1746	2.1412	2.1127	2.1400	2.1131
Sweden	4.5185	4.2871	4.2296	5.0634	6.2826	7.6671
Switzerland	1.788	1.6627	1.6757	1.9642	2.0303	2.0991
UK	0.5200	0.4700	0.4300	0.4930	0.5710	0.6590
US	1.0000	1.0000	1.0000	1.0000	1.0000	1.0000

Table 7.6 Continued

Country	1984	1985	1986	1987	1988	1989
Australia	1.1370	1.4270	1.4910	1.4270	1.2750	1.2620
Austria	20.0090	20.6900	15.2670	12.6430	12.3480	13.2310
Belgium	57.7840	59.3780	44.6720	37.3340	36.7680	39.4040
Canada	1.2951	1.3655	1.3895	1.3260	1.2307	1.1840
China	2.3200	2.9367	3.4528	3.7221	3.7221	4.7221
Denmark	10.3570	10.5960	8.0910	6.8400	6.7315	7.3102
Finland	6.010	6.1979	5.0695	4.3956	4.1828	4.2912
France	8.7391	8.9852	6.9261	6.0107	5.7569	6.3801
Germany	2.8459	2.9440	2.1715	1.7974	1.7562	1.8800
Hong Kong[a]	7.9010	7.7910	7.8030	7.7980	7.8115	7.8083
Italy	1757.0000	1909.4000	1490.8000	1296.1000	1301.6000	1372.1000
Japan	237.5200	238.5400	168.5200	144.6400	128.1500	137.9600
Netherlands	3.2087	3.3214	2.4500	2.0257	1.9766	2.1207
Norway	8.1615	8.5972	7.3947	6.7375	6.5170	6.9045
Singapore	2.1331	2.2002	2.1774	2.1060	2.0124	1.9503
Sweden	8.2718	8.6039	7.1236	6.3404	6.1272	6.4469
Switzerland	2.3497	2.4571	1.7989	1.4912	1.4633	1.6359
UK	0.7480	0.7710	0.6820	0.6100	0.5614	0.6099
US	1.0000	1.0000	1.0000	1.0000	1.0000	1.0000

Notes: [a] Figures for 1978–87 are from the United Nations *Statistical Indicators for Asia and the Pacific*, New York; figures for 1988–9 are from 'Prices and Trends: Currencies,' *Far Eastern Economic Review*, 12 October 1989 and 27 December 1990 indices for China are used (Table 7.5). Consumer price data refer to the cost-of-living index. This index is mainly a weighted average of the retail price index for state-owned commercial enterprises and the price index for the service trade. Agricultural data refer to the index of state purchase prices for agricultural products and by-products. Table 7.5 also provides revised consumer and agricultural price indices for China ((c) and (d)). Using Feltenstein and Farhadian's estimation, changes in these price indices are revised by a factor of 2.5 times the changes in the original indices.

(4) Nominal exchange rates. The nominal exchange rates for China and its eighteen major partners are presented in Table 7.6.

Measurement results

Calculated nominal trade-weighted exchange rates for exports and imports between 1978 and 1987 are reported in Table 7.7. The nominal trade-weighted exchange rate takes only changes in the exchange rates of trading partners into account and does not consider relative price changes. The real effective exchange rates take into account both changes in trading partners' exchange rate and relative prices.

The influence of trading partners' exchange rate changes on the *renminbi* exchange rate can be seen in the nominal trade-weighted exchange rate. Columns (1) and (2) in Table 7.7 show that the official exchange rate appreciated during 1978–80. The corresponding trade-weighted exchange rates for exports and imports were more than the official rate and the *renminbi* actually depreciated in terms of trade weights. The deviations of the trade-weighted exchange rates from the official exchange rate were caused by fluctuations in the exchange rates of the eighteen currencies. Between 1978 and 1980 most trading partners' currencies appreciated (Table 7.6), but the *renminbi* appreciated less than the trading partners' weighted average exchange rate and this caused the *renminbi* trade-weighted exchange rate devaluation in contrast to the official rate appreciation.

The government began to devalue the *renminbi* currency in 1981. Since 1984 the *renminbi* has been devalued rapidly at more than 16 per cent each year. The trade-weighted exchange rates for both exports and imports were higher than the nominal rates during 1981–4, showing that the *renminbi* was devalued more in terms of trade weights. China's trading partners' currencies depreciated

Table 7.7 Nominal trade-weighted exchange rates of China, 1978–89
(renminbi/US$, 1978 = 100)

	Nominal		Nominal trade-weighted exports		Nominal trade-weighted imports	
	rate (1)	index (2)	rate (3)	index (4)	rate (5)	index (6)
1978	1.6836	100.0	1.6836	100.0	1.6836	100.0
1979	1.5550	92.4	1.7324	102.9	1.6903	100.4
1980	1.4984	89.0	1.7392	103.3	1.7038	101.2
1981	1.7045	101.2	1.8688	111.0	1.7863	106.1
1982	1.8925	112.4	2.0456	121.5	1.9294	114.6
1983	1.9757	117.3	2.2224	132.0	2.0489	121.7
1984	2.3200	137.8	2.3200	137.8	2.4160	143.5
1985	2.9367	174.4	2.3099	137.2	2.1920	130.2
1986	3.4528	205.1	2.2038	130.9	2.1281	126.4
1987	3.7221	221.1	3.1466	127.5	1.8856	112.0
1988	3.7221	221.1	2.1348	126.8	1.8789	111.6
1989	4.7221	280.5	2.1971	130.5	1.9580	116.3

Source: Column (1) (nominal exchange rates) are from the IMF, International Financial Statistics, Washington, 1979–90.

Note: Columns (2)–(6) are authors' own calculations Exchange rate indices are calculated from exchange rate levels. Nominal trade-weighted exchange rates for exports and imports are calculated using export- and import-weighted average exchange rates of China's eighteen trading partners

between 1981 and 1985. Among the eighteen partners, sixteen currencies (all except the Singapore dollar and Japanese yen) depreciated. However, the weighted average exchange rate of partner countries depreciated less than the renminbi devaluation between 1981–4 and this resulted in higher values of trade-weighted exchange rates for China than official rates.

The trade-weighted exchange rate for both exports and imports showed an appreciation in 1985. Despite a devaluation of 36.6 per cent in 1985, the renminbi was still devalued by less than the trading partners' weighted average exchange rate depreciation. During 1986–9, most currencies (with the exception of the Australian dollar in 1986, Canadian dollar in 1986, Hong Kong dollar in 1986 and 1988 and the Italian lira in 1988 and 1989) appreciated. This caused China's trade-weighted exchange rates to appreciate and their values were lower than the official rates. Although there was a trade-weighted exchange rate devaluation in 1989, both export- and import-weighted exchange rates were still lower than the official rate, demonstrating a smaller devaluation in terms of trade weights.

Comparing the export-weighted exchange rate with the import-weighted rate, the exchange rates for exports were usually higher than those for imports (except for 1984), implying that the exchange rate was devalued more in terms of export weights than in terms of import weights.

Tables 7.8 and 7.9 give the real effective exchange rates for exports and imports. The real effective exchange rates in columns (3)–(4) and (5)–(6) are calculated using the official consumer and wholesale price indices, while those in columns (7)–(8) and (9)–(10) are based on revised price indices. A lower real exchange rate relative to the nominal rate often indicates higher domestic inflation than in the trading partners' economies and the impact of devaluation is modified by such inflation. A higher measure of inflation is recorded in the official wholesale price index than in the official consumer price index, and in the revised price indices than in the official price indices. Thus, the real effective exchange rates in terms of the wholesale price index and revised indices are much

Table 7.8 The real effective trade-weighted exchange rates for exports, 1978–89 (renminbi/US$, 1978 = 100)

	Nominal		Real based on CPI		Real based on API		Real based on revised CPI		Real based on revised API	
	rate (1)	index (2)	rate (3)	index (4)	rate (5)	index (6)	rate (7)	index (8)	rate (9)	index (10)
1978	1.6836	100.0	1.6836	100.0	1.6836	100.0	1.6836	100.0	1.6836	100.0
1979	1.5550	92.4	1.8755	111.4	1.5657	93.0	1.8233	108.3	1.2324	73.2
1980	1.4984	89.0	2.0170	119.8	1.6870	100.2	1.7846	106.0	1.2459	74.0
1981	1.7045	101.2	2.3150	137.5	1.8755	111.4	1.9883	118.1	1.3233	78.6
1982	1.8925	112.4	2.6584	157.9	2.1516	127.8	2.2325	132.6	1.5152	90.0
1983	1.9757	117.3	3.0355	180.3	3.4188	142.5	2.4951	148.2	1.6146	95.9
1984	2.3200	137.8	3.2914	195.5	2.5692	152.6	2.6332	156.4	1.6853	100.1
1985	2.9367	174.4	3.0322	180.1	2.4294	144.3	2.1988	130.6	1.5169	90.1
1986	3.4528	205.1	2.8638	170.1	2.2846	135.7	1.9850	117.9	1.3553	80.5
1987	3.7221	221.1	2.9059	172.6	2.2240	132.1	1.9176	113.9	1.2728	75.6
1988	3.7221	221.1	2.4075	143.0	2.0355	120.9	1.4210	84.4	1.1179	66.4
1989	4.7221	280.5	2.3217	137.9	—	—	1.2846	76.3	—	—

Source: Nominal exchange rates are from the IMF, *International Financial Statistics*, Washington, 1979–90.

Note: The real effective exchange rate indices are calculated according to equation (2). The real effective exchange rate levels are caculated from the real effective exchange rate indices.

Table 7.9 The real effective trade-weighted exchange rates for imports, 1978–89 (renminbi/US$, 1978 = 100)

	Nominal		Real based on CPI		Real based on API		Real based on revised CPI		Real based on revised API	
	rate (1)	index (2)	rate (3)	index (4)	rate (5)	index (6)	rate (7)	index (8)	rate (9)	index (10)
1978	1.6836	100.0	1.6836	100.0	1.6836	100.0	1.6836	100.0	1.6836	100.0
1979	1.5550	92.4	1.8351	109.0	1.5321	91.0	1.7829	105.9	1.2038	71.5
1980	1.4984	89.0	1.9631	116.6	1.6432	97.6	1.7375	103.2	1.2139	72.1
1981	1.7045	101.2	2.1483	127.6	1.7408	103.4	1.8452	109.6	1.2273	72.9
1982	1.8925	112.4	2.4176	143.6	1.9563	116.2	2.0304	120.6	1.3772	81.8
1983	1.9757	117.3	2.6146	155.3	2.0658	122.7	2.1483	127.6	1.3907	82.6
1984	2.3200	137.8	3.1197	185.3	2.4345	144.6	2.4951	148.2	1.5961	94.8
1985	2.9367	174.4	2.5961	154.2	2.0809	123.6	1.8823	111.8	1.2981	77.1
1986	3.4528	205.1	2.4193	143.7	1.9311	114.7	1.6769	99.6	1.1651	69.2
1987	3.7221	221.1	2.2947	136.3	1.7560	104.3	1.5152	90.0	1.0051	59.7
1988	3.7221	221.1	1.9361	115.0	1.6365	97.2	1.1432	67.9	0.8990	53.4
1989	4.7221	280.5	1.8806	111.7	—	—	1.0405	61.8	—	—

Source: Nominal exchange rates are from the IMF, *International Financial Statistics*, Washington, 1979–90.

Note: The real effective exchange rate indices are calculated according to equation (2). The real effective exchange rate levels are calculated from the real effective exchange rate indices.

lower than the real rates based on the consumer price index and the official price indices.

Despite an appreciation of the nominal exchange rate during 1978–80, the measures based on the official price indices and revised consumer price indices indicate a real devaluation for both export- and import-weighted exchange rates, that is, higher real effective exchange rates than nominal rates. This occurred because price inflation, as measured by these three indices, was lower than the price inflation experienced by China's trading partners at that time. The measure based on the revised wholesale price indices demonstrated a real appreciation.

During 1981–4, the *renminbi* devaluation was accompanied by domestic inflation which was slightly lower than the inflation between 1985 and 1989. In the case of the official and revised consumer price indices, the real effective exchange rates were higher than the nominal rates. All real indices show a depreciation over the period. Due to the higher inflation prevailing in the economies of China's trading partners at that time and higher real exchange rates for exports than for imports, the *renminbi* devaluation had a real effect on the country's foreign trade.

The Chinese economy experienced high inflation during 1985–9 and this is reflected in the trend of the real effective exchange rates. In 1985 the real effective exchange rates for both exports and imports began to show an appreciation. The value of the real exchange rate based on the official consumer price index was still higher than the nominal rate in 1985, but from 1986 the real exchange rates based on all the official and revised price indices had lower values, indicating a real overvaluation. The real appreciation implies that the nominal exchange rate devaluations were insignificant during this period because they were offset by higher domestic inflation in China than in the economies of China's trading partners, so that the real exchange rate actually appreciated rather than depreciated.

This result is quite different from the World Bank's conclusion that China's real exchange rate depreciated by as much as 100 per cent between 1978 and 1988, assisting export growth.[42] The real exchange rate used in the World Bank study was calculated in terms of composite foreign trade. In this study the real exchange rate for imports and exports is considered separately. This is not the reason for the different results between the two studies, however, because · the real exchange rates for imports and exports in this study have shown the same trend and direction. In its estimation the World Bank used two sets of price indices: wholesale prices of trading partners compared with China's consumer prices, and consumer prices of trading partners compared with China's consumer prices. This is not very different from the price indices used in this chapter.

The main reason for the contradictory conclusions appears to be the use of different definitions of real exchange rates. The World Bank defined the real effective exchange rate as

$$\text{REER} = \frac{(\text{NBERS}/\text{PI})}{\Sigma(\text{NBERS}j/\text{PI}'j)a_j} \tag{3}$$

where

NBERS = nominal bilateral exchange rate of Chinese *renminbi* per US $

NBERSj = nominal bilateral exchange rate of jth trading partner of China

PI = price index for China

PI'j = price index of China's j^{th} trading partner

a_j = trade weights (using top ten trading partners' exports and imports averaged over 1984–6)

If trade weights are not taken into account, equation (3) can be simplified into a real bilateral exchange rate with the following form:

$$REER = \frac{NBERS \cdot PI'_j}{NBERS_j \cdot PI} \tag{4}$$

The World Bank's results show a decreasing trend for the real effective exchange rate during 1978–88, particularly after 1980. According to equations (3) and (4), however, a decrease in the value of the real effective exchange rate REER should be interpreted as appreciation rather than depreciation because the World Bank defined NBERS and NBERS$_j$ as nominal exchange rates for China and trading partners per US dollar. In equations (3) and (4) a decrease in REER means that a unit of China's trading partners' currency can exchange for less *renminbi*. Therefore, the World Bank's estimates actually have the same directions as this study indicates. The only difference is that the World Bank has not interpreted its results accordingly. Thus, its conclusion that 'over the last decade China's real effective exchange rate has depreciated significantly'[43] seems questionable. It is unrealistic to expect a significant real devaluation in a country with severe price inflation as was the case for China between 1985 and 1989. The results of this study support that.

4 CONCLUSIONS

With the re-orientation of its economic development strategy to an 'open door' policy, China has become more outward-looking with an increasing share of foreign trade in GNP and the utilisation of foreign funds, including private direct foreign investment. Simultaneously, despite the continuation of planning and other forms of direct intervention in the economy, the country has moved toward a more market-oriented system. The reduction of export subsidies and the opening of foreign exchange swap centres have been some of the measures taken. Foreign exchange swap centres have become, in a limited form, China's secondary foreign exchange market. With the co-existence of the official exchange rate and secondary market exchange rate, a dual exchange rate regime has been adopted in China. For foreign exchange allocation, a retention system has been introduced in export enterprises to distribute foreign exchange earnings between the central government and enterprises or local governments. These changes involved use of the exchange rate as a policy instrument, particularly during the 1990s.

The exchange rate was rigid before 1989. Despite the sharp devaluations at the end of 1989 and 1990, there was still some overvaluation in terms of unit costs of foreign exchange earnings. The estimates of real effective exchange rates for imports and exports in this chapter indicate that China's real effective exchange rate depreciated insignificantly during 1985–9 because of the existence of high domestic inflation.

Given the changeability of world markets and the complexity of the domestic economy, it is difficult for the Chinese government to determine the exchange rate in a simple mechanical manner. There is more scope for the exchange rate to be determined by market forces. As a result, a more flexible exchange rate policy should be adopted. Under the present circumstances of a financially repressed economy, the exchange rate could be adjusted in sympathy with the rate of inflation to minimise the 'necessary' rate of price inflation. Furthermore, a convertible *renminbi* currency and a floating exchange rate system should ultimately be adopted in China so as to fully link the domestic economy with world markets and provide greater scope for the exchange rate to be used as a policy instrument.

Exchange controls, including quantitative restrictions, cause serious price distortions and strongly affect the consequences of foreign exchange policy. Removing these controls to reduce bias against exports should thus be a requirement of first-best policy and is necessary for the long-run success of the economic reform programme in China.

As one of the components of exchange control, the dual exchange rate regime is not consistent with further economic development. It has been argued by many observers[44] that the exchange rate should be unified in a financially repressed economy to ease (at least partially) the pressure of inflation. If the move to a more market-oriented economy is to be successful, there is a need for a unified exchange rate.

Tarr[45] estimated the effects of Poland's foreign exchange policies on welfare under different exporter retention rates of foreign exchange earnings. His result showed that full retention by exporters in the absence of other distortions would provide social benefits equivalent to 8 per cent of GDP. In the presence of distortions, however, the net effect of full retention with other policies together would be a bias toward tradables. In another study within the context of a general equilibrium model for China, Gao[46] found that an increase in each export good's retention rate combined with an exchange rate devaluation would increase exports, imports and GDP but cause higher inflation rates. Considering these empirical results and a 40 per cent retention of foreign exchange by enterprises, a further increase in the retention rate for general export goods, but somewhat less than full retention, is needed as a second best foreign exchange policy to stimulate exports at an overvalued exchange rate.

Effects of foreign exchange policy can be influenced by either price inflation or the structure of the price system. In the dual price system, primary goods are priced at relatively low levels and manufactures at relatively high levels. As a result of the biased price structure, foreign trade enterprises have earned distorted profits and losses from some exports and imports. This in turn leads to dislocation of trade structure and whittles down the positive effects of foreign exchange policy.

In order to derive positive effects from foreign exchange policy, the government has to pay more attention to maintaining domestic prices at a low level and prevent agents and units from raising their product prices. The price structure must be reformed. The fundamental aim of reforming the present price system and maintaining price stability should be to unify the dual price system and further free up domestic prices.

Fiscal policy plays an important role in creating a sound macroeconomic environment within which foreign exchange policy can be pursued. The adjustment processes of the 1980s demonstrated that subsidies were costly to the budget. Despite the abolition of export subsidies in 1991, import subsidies have been maintained. In order to relieve the burden on the budget and to enhance competitiveness, import subsidies must be removed. This could be done gradually taking export costs into consideration. Concerns about increases in export costs and losses in international competitiveness can be relieved by import liberalising measures, price reforms and policies encouraging enterprise productivity improvement.

As a component of budget reforms, appropriate policies must be formulated to increase the country's budget income. Reform in the fiscal system is to remove the 'one big rice bowl' mentality of enterprises and units and implement more efficient management through adoption of market mechanisms in place of administrative controls.

APPENDIX: REFORMS AND EVENTS IN THE FOREIGN TRADE AND FOREIGN EXCHANGE SYSTEM SINCE 1979

1979   Foreign trade management was decentralised from the central Ministry of Foreign Economic Relations and Trade to a number of coastal provinces and municipalities and a few selected central, industrial ministries.

The Customs Office was separated from the central Ministry of Foreign Relations and Trade and granted independent administrative status under the State Council.

1.1.79   A local retention system for foreign exchange earnings from exports was introduced.
Features: the system was based on areas and the fulfilment of export plans.
Purpose: to create an incentive for exports.
Effects: export incentive; decentralisation of foreign trade, particularly in the area of imports.

1980   Tariffs and industrial and commercial taxes for exports and imports were reduced.
Purpose: to use tariffs and tax exemptions as an indirect means of regulating foreign trade.

Special economic zones in Guangdong· and Fujian provinces were established.
Purpose: to make the two provinces the forerunners of a new industrialisation strategy based on export promotion and foreign investment.

1.1.81   An internal exchange rate regime for foreign trade was implemented.
Features: internal settlement rates for foreign trade set at 2.80 *renminbi* per US dollar; the official exchange rate for non-tradable goods kept at 1.53 *renminbi* per US dollar.

Purposes: to create incentives for exports and restrict imports; to avoid losses from non-tradable goods.
Effects: export incentives; a dual exchange rate regime established.

1982 New limitations on financial subsidies for export losses were introduced.
Features: subsidies limited to losses within the limits of approved costs.
Purpose: to put institutional pressure on provincial management of foreign trade.
Effects: export expansion.

1984 Foreign trade management was further decentralised.
Features: administrative departments at all levels were not allowed to interfere with the special business of foreign trade enterprises; the enterprises were to conduct import-export business independently, keeping their own accounts and bearing responsibility for the profits and losses of their operation.

State control over foreign trade was liberalised.
Features: enterprises that had not undertaken foreign trade activities were allowed to do so either with approval from the central and provincial authorities, or via the new system of export and import agencies.
Purposes: to further liberalise trade; to abandon the institutional barriers that had separated domestic prices from international prices.

Existing import and export controls and restrictions were relaxed.

The local retention system was redefined.
Features: different retention rates for different localities: special economic zones, 100 per cent; autonomous regions of nationalities, 50 per cent; Guangdong and Fujian (special policy status), 30 per cent; other provinces, 25 per cent.
Purpose: to encourage exports from special economic zones.
Effects: export incentives for special economic zones; a

better position for special economic zones *vis-à-vis* unequal competition; domestic price increases; import increases.

12.1.84 The internal settlement rate was abolished.
Causes: export cost increases arising from domestic price inflation and the liberalisation of the procurement prices of many exportable goods; attempts to remove foreign trade subsidies.

4.1.85 The subsidy system for exports was re-introduced.

1985 Restrictive policies toward imports were strengthened.
Features: an increase in import duties and the imposition of adjustment taxes on imported goods that had been sold with a high profit margin in the domestic market.

A general rationalisation and re-shuffling of the newly established local and central foreign trade enterprises took place.

Constraints were introduced on the use of retained foreign exchange earnings held by local authorities and enterprises.
Purpose: to reverse the tendency for a rapid draining of the foreign exchange reserves.

1986 The *renminbi* was devalued to 3.72 *renminbi* per US dollar.
Purpose: to create further export incentives.

Additional bonuses for the overfulfilment of export plans were introduced.
Purpose: to create further export incentives.

Heavily regulated local markets for foreign exchange in special economic zones were established.
Purposes: to act as competition for black markets; to further devalue the *renminbi* in special economic zones.

1987 A comprehensive contract responsibility system for re-centralising the entire foreign trade system adopted by the Ministry of Foreign Economic Relations and Trade.
Features: the contracts signed between the Ministry of Foreign Economic Relations and Trade and the State Council and between different levels of trading corporations obliged them to fulfil three planned targets: export

volume, level of export costs and efficiency in export management.

1988   The recentralised monopoly over foreign trade held by the Ministry of Foreign Economic Relations and Trade was removed.

Features: decentralisation of foreign trade management to provincial authorities; adoption of a system of responsibility contracts for exports signed between the State Council and provincial governments and between different levels of territorial administration, trading corporations and enterprises, the contract system allowing provincial authorities to further decentralise foreign trade management to sub-provincial authorities and to corporations and enterprises.

An experiment was conducted in three industries: garments, light industries and arts and crafts.

Features: the share accruing to exporters in the foreign exchange retention system was increased to a standard rate of 75 per cent, export subsidies were abolished and financial and economic independence granted to exporting corporations and enterprises.

Purpose: to bring additional *renminbi* revenue to exporters to compensate for possible losses due to high export costs.

1.1..88   The local retention system was modified.

Features: more attention to product structure: an 80 per cent retention ratio for special economic zones instead of the 100 per cent ratio; an increase in the retention ratio for the three selected industries to 80 per cent for all localities; a 100 per cent ratio for electrical equipment and machinery for all localities.

Purpose: to remove an important element of unequal competition in the market of exportable goods procurement.

1988   More foreign exchange swap centres were set up and the restrictive controls over these centres were liberalised.

Purpose: to create a foreign exchange market.

12.1989 The *renminbi* was devalued by 21 per cent to 4.7221 *renminbi* per US dollar.

11.1.90 The *renminbi* was devalued by 9 per cent to 5.1831 *renminbi* per US dollar.

1.1991 Reforms in the foreign trade system were further introduced.

Features: comprehensive implementation of losses-profits responsibility in foreign trade enterprises; the abolition of export subsidies; the adjustment of retention rates with a general increase for local enterprises to 50 per cent.

Purposes: to reduce budgetary burden; to vitalise enterprises and increase exports.

Notes

1 The World Bank presented a series of substantive research reports on China's economic reforms: World Bank, *China: Long-Term Issues and Options*, Main Report, Washington, DC 1985; *China: The Energy Sector*, Washington, DC, 1985; *China: Economic Model and Projections*, World Bank Report, Washington, DC, 1985; *China: Economic Structure in International Perspective*, Washington, DC, 1985; *China: External Trade and Capital*, Washington, DC, 1988; *China: Macroeconomic Stability and Industrial Growth under Decentralized Socialism*, World Bank Country Study, Washington, DC, 1990. Tam (1987) analysed China's foreign exchange controls; Chan reviewed reform measures relating to foreign trade and the exchange system between 1979 and 1986; Hsu (1989) investigated the impact of China's foreign trade reforms on growth and stability: O. K. (1987) Tam, 'Issues in Foreign Exchange Control in China'. Paper presented at an International Workshop on the Economic Relationship between Australia, China and Japan, the Australia–Japan Research Centre, Australian National University, September; T. Chan, (1989) 'China's Foreign Exchange and Trade Controls: What Next?' Paper presented at a seminar held by the Centre for Chinese Political Economy, Macquarie University, New South Wales, Australia (mimeo); J. Hsu, (1989) *China's Foreign Trade Reforms: Impact on Growth and Stability*, Cambridge University Press, Cambridge.
2 Tam (1987).
3 State Bureau of Statistics, *Statistical Yearbook of China, 1989*, p. 633.
4 Chan (1989).
5 The Ministry of Foreign Economic Relations and Trade, *Statistical Yearbook of China, 1989*.
6 T. Zheng (1987) 'The Problem of Reforming China's Foreign Trade System', *Chinese Economic Studies*, Summer: pp. 27–49.
7 N. Vousden (1990) *The Economics of Trade Protection*, Cambridge Uni-

versity Press, Cambridge. E. Helpman and P. R. Krugman (1989) *Trade Policy and Market Structure*, MIT Press, Cambridge Mass.

8 *Statistical Yearbook of China*, p. 673.

9 The Ministry of Foreign Economic Relations and Trade (1987a) 'Major Policy Choices in the Foreign Trade Reform'. Prepared for the State Council of China, Unpublished.

10 The Research Centre for Economic, Technological and Social Development, State Council, 1990, No. 6; *Almanac of China's Finance and Banking*, 1989, p. 44.

11 Y. Xue (1989) 'Strengthening Foreign Exchange Controls in Adjustment', *Chinese Finance*, pp. 94–95.

12 Chan (1989).

13 Chan (1989), p. 7.

14 D. Zhao (1989) 'Trade and Industry Reform and Policy Research in China'. Paper presented to the Senior Policy Seminar on Managing Trade and Industry Reforms in Asia: The Role of Policy Research, Canberra (mimeo), No. 50.

15 *Light Industry Yearbook of China*, 1988.

16 Chan (1989), pp. 15, 20.

17 The Research Centre for Economic, Technological and Social Development, State Council, P. R. China, 1990. 'A Review of China's International Financial System and Policy During the Last Decade', *Working Paper* No. 4.

18 China Trade Report, 21/1/1991.

19 Tam (1987).

20 In Guangdong province, for instance, 60 per cent of units have less than US$1,000, and some have only a couple of US$10 (The Research Centre for Economic, Technological and Social Development, State Council, 1990).

21 G. Chang (1987) 'Frailties of a Fake Forex Market', *International Trade*, February: 27.

22 G. Zhang (1990) 'A Review and Outlook of China's Foreign Exchange Adjustment Market', *Finance Study*, Vol. 9: pp. 1–5.

23 Zhang (1990).

24 The Research Centre for Economic, Technological and Social Development, State Council, 1990, No. 4.

25 Q. Jiao (1989) 'The Formation and Development of a Foreign Exchange Adjustment Market', *International Finance Study*, Vol. 9: pp. 38–41.

26 C. Xiao (1989) 'Should the *Renminbi* Exchange Rate Against US Dollar be Adjusted and How to Adjust It?' *International Finance Study*, Vol. 11: pp. 15–17.

27 J. Xing (1987) 'The Objectives and Ways for the Implementation of Opening Up the Foreign Exchange Market', *Financial Study (Jinrong Yanjiu)*, No. 6: pp. 54–56.

28 Y. Chen (1987) 'Some Suggestions to Avoid Losses from Exchange Rate Changes', *Financial Times (Jinrong Shibao)*, 23 July: p. 3.

29 Xing (1987) p. 55.

30 Jiao (1989).

31 *People's Daily*, 14 February 1989.
32 *People's Daily*, 14 February 1989.
33 G. Zhang (1990) pp. 1–5.
34 B. Chen and C. Yang (1990) 'An Analysis of the Effects of Exchange Rate Adjustments on the Machinery and Electronic Product Markets', *Zhongguo Wujia (China Prices)*, August: pp. 49–51.
35 A. Krueger (1978) *Liberalization Attempts and Consequences*, Ballinger, Cambridge, Mass.; M. Khan and P. Montiel (1987) 'Real Exchange Rate Dynamics in a Small, Primary-export Country', *International Monetary Fund Staff Papers*, Vol. 34: pp. 681–710.; A. Harberger (1986) 'Economic Adjustment and the Real Exchange Rate', in S. Edwards and L. Ahamed (eds), *Economic Adjustment and Exchange Rates in Developing Countries*, University of Chicago Press, Chicago: pp. 371–414.
36 M. Bruno (1976) 'The Two-sector Open Economy and the Real Exchange Rate', *The American Economic Review*, Vol. 66, September, pp. 566–577; R. Dornbusch (1974) 'Tariffs and Nontraded Goods', *Journal of International Economics*, Vol. 4: pp. 117–185; R. Dornbusch (1980) *Open Economy Macroeconomics*, Basic Books, New York; S. Edwards (1989) 'Real Change Rates in the Developing Countries: Concepts and Measurement', *NBER Working Paper*, No. 2950; A. Krueger (1978) *Liberalisation Attempts and Consequences*, Ballinger, Cambridge, Mass.; A. Krueger (1983) *Exchange Rate Determination*, Cambridge University Press, Cambridge; M. Mussa (1984) 'The Theory of Exchange Rate Determination', in J. Bilson and R. Marston (eds), *Exchange Rate Theory and Practice*, University of Chicago Press, Chicago.
37 Edwards (1989), No. 4.
38 J. Artus (1978) 'Methods of Assessing the Long-run Equilibrium Value of an Exchange rate', *Journal of International Economics*, Vol. 8: pp. 277–299; J. Artus and M. Knight (1984) 'Issues in the Assessment of the Exchange Rate in Industrial Countries', *IMF Occasional Paper*, no. 29, Washington, DC; S. Edwards (1989); J. Frenkel (1978) 'Purchasing Power Parity: Doctrinal Perspectives and Evidence From the 1920s', *Journal of International Economics*, Vol. 8: pp. 169–191; H. Genberg (1978) 'Purchasing Power Parity under Fixed and Flexible Exchange Rates', *Journal of International Economics*, Vol. 18: pp. 321–338; L. Officer (1982) *Purchasing Power Parity and Exchange Rates: Theory, Evidence and Relevance, Contemporary Studies in Economic and Financial Analysis* No. 35, JAI Press; P. Maciejewski (1983) 'Real Effective Exchange Rate Indexes: A Re-examination of the Major Conceptual and Methodological issues', *IMF Staff Papers*, Vol. 30: pp. 491–541.
39 IMF (1989) *International Financial Statistics*, No. 12.
40 Edwards (1989), No. 78.
41 A. Feltenstein and Z. Farhadian (1987) 'Fiscal Policy, Monetary Targets, and the Price Level in a Centrally Planned Economy: An Application to the Case of China', *Journal of Money, Credit, and Banking*, Vol. 19, No. 2: pp. 137–156. They estimated China's inflation rate between 1954 and 1983 with the result that 'the true rate of inflation

was determined to be approximately 2.5 times the official rate' p. 153 during this period.

42 World Bank, 1990, No. 24.

43 World Bank, 1990, No. 23.

44 See, for example, McKinnon, R. I. (1979) *Money in International Exchange: The Convertible Currency System* (New York: Oxford University Press); McKinnon, R. I. (1992) *The Order of Economic Liberalization: Financial Control in the Transition to a Market Economy* (Baltimore: Johns Hopkins University Press); McKinnon and Donald (1981); Tam (1987); Zhang (1990).

45 D. Tarr (1990) 'Second-best Foreign Exchange Policy in the Presence of Domestic Price Controls and Export Subsidies', *The World Bank Economic Review* Vol. 4, No. 2, pp. 175–194.

46 Gao (1992).

INDEX

Agricultural Bank of China (ABC) 1, 58, 107, 116, 132
Agricultural Development Bank of China (ADBC), 131, 132, 133, 134
agricultural policy loans 132, 133
Ahamed, L. 187
appreciation of the exchange rate 174, 178
Artus, J. 187
Asian Development Bank 170
Associated Village Credit Co-operatives 134
austerity programs 65
autonomy of foreign trade enterprises 147
average cost of foreign exchange earnings 152

balance of budgets 12
bank capital 17, 87
bank concentration 58
bank credit maturity 108
bank credits and policy 13, 17, 25, 30, 32, 61, 70, 126
bank deposits 33
bank deposits composition 18, 33
Bank Governors' Meeting 63
Bank of China 86, 113, 116, 147, 158
Bank of Communications 113
bank reserves 15, 40
banking system: independence and autonomy 5, 6, 40, 46, 121, 123,

129; source of budget revenues 42; administrative role 59; blind expansion 124; monobanking system 6, 11, 62, 85; regionalisation 95, 123; public ownership 129; specialised banks 34, 41, 46, 57, 125; enterprisation 57, 68, 91, 101, 111, 128, 129; retention of after-tax profit 120, 121; solvency 70, 71, 125; profit 42, 126; supervisory role 129
bank bond issues 16, 17
bank reform 46, 47
banks' liabilitites to international financial institutions 17
Barnett, W.A. 50
Bilson, J. 187
Board of Directors and Supervisory Committee of Rural Credit Co-operatives 137
Bordo, M.D. 50
Bruno, M. 187
budget deficit 1, 25, 26
Budget Imbalance Contribution Index 26, 52
budget targets 26
business scope of financial institutions 117
Byrd, W. 48

Capital Construction Finance Department 85
capital market 42, 57

189